Foreword

Since recommendations were made by HMIC in the early 1990s, most forces in England and Wales have either established specialist domestic violence units, or have employed specialist domestic violence officers in some other capacity. A considerable amount of work has been done looking at how police forces respond to and deal with victims and offenders in domestic violence incidents, but comparatively little research has addressed how forces are organised to deliver this service.

This is important as the type of organisation in place can ultimately affect the quality of service which forces provide when dealing with domestic violence. It also greatly affects the experience of those officers who work in this area, what their job entails and the degree to which they can provide a valuable service as efficiently and effectively as possible.

This report looks at the role of the specialist domestic violence officer, their location within force structures, the practices in place for monitoring performance, and the way in which information on incidents is communicated between officers. It will help forces identify good practice and areas for improvement in the types of organisational structure for dealing with domestic violence. It also provides information for other agencies to consider in improving service delivery in this important area.

Dr Gloria Laycock
Head of Policing and Reducing Crime Unit
Research, Development and Statistics Directorate
Home Office
December 1998

Acknowledgements

Thanks are due to all members of the police service who participated in this study and were so generous with their time and expertise.

Two former police officers contributed significantly to the research: Elaine Morrison, who carried out many of the interviews, and Margaret Dodgson, who provided advice at the early stages. Their assistance was invaluable.

Superintendent David Cox, HM Inspectorate of Constabulary, provided an overview of police policy and practice. Superintendent Andrew Tyrrell permitted us to take part in domestic violence courses at Bramshill Police Staff College. Colonel Margaret Patten provided information about the innovative procedures of the Baltimore Police Department.

Gary Mundy, Jonathan Nicholls and Jacqueline Russell of the Policing and Reducing Crime Unit provided helpful advice at all stages of the project.

The authors

Joyce Plotnikoff and Richard Woolfson are independent consultants in management, IT and the law.

PRCU would like to thank Professor Janet Walker, Relate Centre for Family Studies, University of Newcastle upon Tyne, for acting as independent assessor for this report.

Police Research Series
Paper 100

Policing Domestic Violence: Effective Organisational Structures

Joyce Plotnikoff
Richard Woolfson

LEARNING RESOURC
CENTRE
Havering College
of Further and Higher Education

Editor: Barry Webb
Home Office
Policing and Reducing Crime Unit
Research, Development and Statistics Directorate
50 Queen Anne's Gate
London SW1H 9AT

RDS
Research Development Statistics

262·82

4742

Policing and Reducing Crime Unit: Police Research Series

The Policing and Reducing Crime Unit (PRC Unit) was formed in 1998 as a result of the merger of the Police Research Group (PRG) and the Research and Statistics Directorate. The PRC Unit is now one part of the Research, Development and Statistics Directorate of the Home Office. The PRC Unit carries out and commissions research in the social and management sciences on policing and crime reduction, broadening the role that PRG played.

The PRC Unit has now combined PRG's two main series into the Police Research Series, continuing PRG's earlier work. This series will present research material on crime prevention and detection as well as police management and organisation issues.

Research commissioned by PRG will appear as a PRC Unit publication. Throughout the text there may be references to PRG and these now need to be understood as relating to the PRC Unit.

ISBN 1-84082-205-8

Copies of this publication can be made available in formats accessible to the visually impaired on request.

Executive summary

Previous work on domestic violence has tended to focus on either the nature of the police response to incidents, or victim support issues. This study seeks to add to knowledge of how the police are organised internally (i.e. the systems and structures in place) to provide a service dealing specifically with domestic violence incidents.

The study was undertaken in three phases between August 1997 and March 1998; 42 of the 43 forces in England and Wales participated.

The main areas investigated are organisational in nature. This organisation is important as it determines the extent to which forces can provide an efficient and effective service for dealing with domestic violence. Issues such as whether forces have specialist domestic violence officers (DVOs), the scope of their role, and their position within the force are examined as factors which affect service provision. Additional factors, such as how performance is monitored and how information is passed from front-line officers to specialist DVOs, are also identified as influential in determining both the nature of the response provided and the day-to-day work of the DVO.

The main findings were in the following areas:

- Wide variations were found in the scope and content of force policies on domestic violence. Definitions of domestic violence differed, making direct comparisons of performance difficult.

- Domestic incidents involving police officers, either as victims or offenders, presented problems for DVOs. Guidance on dealing with such issues was addressed in only one force.

- Ranges of organisational models for the delivery of a response to domestic violence were found. However, no single structure emerged as either more or less problematic than others. Problems related less to the structure than to the status of domestic violence work within forces and the level of commitment from headquarters and divisional commanders.

- Line management of DVOs was often blurred, leaving some specialist officers feeling isolated within the force structure.

- There was no standard model for the DVO role. A wide spectrum of activities was represented. DVOs often felt that the position was not sufficiently integrated into mainstream policing and that too much of the responsibility for delivery of force policy had fallen on them personally.

- The study found little systematic performance monitoring of the role of the DVO.

- Standards of performance monitoring were generally poor, both for patterns of offending behaviour and quality of police response. Even where statistics were collected, they were little used. There was little attempt to monitor the quality of service provided to victims or the effectiveness with which the different police functions worked together, even though DVOs reported that most problems occurred at these interfaces.

- Forces lacked a systematic approach to the management of information relating to domestic violence incidents, leading to under-counting of them. DVOs spent excessive amounts of their time seeking information rather than responding to it.

- Information about previous incidents at the address, or about domestic violence 'markers' on the command and control system, were not routinely passed on to responding officers.

- DVO records were seldom accessible by other officers which undermined their general intelligence potential.

- Domestic violence was not included in the indicators used by most forces to measure performance, contributing to the perceived low status of this area of police work.

- Despite close links between the two areas, domestic violence and child protection indices were rarely integrated.

- DVOs in some areas were left to exercise their own judgement about whether to tell social workers about children in households where domestic violence incidents were reported. The criteria for referral were seldom incorporated into inter-agency agreements.

- The Home Office key performance indicator on repeat victimisation emphasises the importance of addressing this issue as an integral part of a force crime reduction strategy and is clearly relevant to domestic violence. Repeat victimisation is, to some degree, currently monitored by 60% of forces, although there was widespread concern about the extent to which current systems could accurately and quickly identify repeat incidents. The term 'repeat victimisation' was interpreted in different ways.

● Training on domestic violence should be both systematic and targeted appropriately at both junior officers and senior officers with a key role in the force's response to domestic violence. However, coherent training strategies were not in place. Much of the training had been developed on an ad hoc basis.

On the basis of these key findings, a series of recommendations has been drawn up for consideration by the Home Office, force headquarters, divisional commanders and HMIC. These are contained in section 9 of the report.

Contents

List of figures

List of tables

1. Introduction

Background

In the last decade, the police response to domestic violence incidents has come under increasing criticism. Common criticisms were that incidents were not being taken seriously and were seen as civil rather than criminal matters and that inadequate recording practices obscured a true picture of the extent of domestic violence[1].

During the early 1990s, the Home Office, together with the police service, introduced measures to respond to these criticisms. Home Office Circular 60/1990 emphasised the need for:

- policy documents and clear strategies for dealing with domestic violence incidents;
- an interventionist approach based on the presumption of arrest when an offence has been committed;
- a recording process for 'domestic' incidents which reflects procedures for other violent crimes; and
- the establishment of dedicated units or specialist officers to deal with domestic violence incidents.

Five years later, Grace (1995) noted that although most forces had introduced policies to deal with these needs, the translation of policy into practice had been less successful.

Whereas previous work has focused on the nature and effectiveness of the policing response and victim support, Grace raised issues relating the effective policing of domestic violence incidents to internal force structures, procedures and resourcing provisions. In most areas, the police service was found wanting. This study focuses on these internal force structures and procedures.

Aims

This study aimed to:

- identify the range and respective strengths and weaknesses of the various organisational structures and processes for responding to domestic violence in place in different forces; and
- consider the extent to which forces adopt different roles in respect to policing domestic violence.

[1] *See Edwards, 1986; Smith, 1989; Morley and Mullender, 1994.*

The specific issues examined during the study were:

- the manner in which domestic violence was addressed in force policy documents;
- the range of organisational structures adopted and their perceived effectiveness;
- the nature and scope of the role of specialist domestic violence officers and their line management;
- information management, including communication between different parts of the force;
- the use of monitoring; and
- the provision of training.

Methodology

[2] One force felt unable to participate due to the small size of its resident population.

42 of the 43 forces in England and Wales participated in the study which was undertaken in 3 phases between August 1997 and March 1998.[2] The first phase consisted of a national survey of force organisational structures, data recording, and training and multi-agency work. Copies of force policies and other relevant documentation were also collected.

The second phase focused on all participating forces. Interviews were held with:

- 41 officers responsible for domestic violence policy;
- 40 line managers; and
- 83 operational officers dealing with domestic violence on a daily basis.

Of the 83 operational officers:

- 15 (18%) had been in the post for less than one year;
- 56 (68%) had been in post for between one and three years; and
- 12 (14%) had been in post for longer.

The third phase consisted of visits to five police forces, each with a different organisational approach. Interviews were conducted in a total of 12 divisions, seven control rooms and, where appropriate, with headquarters personnel. A total of 54 interviews were conducted with commanders or members of the command team, DVOs, child protection officers, line managers, control room supervisors and uniform patrol officers.

Structure of the report

The structure of this report reflects the focus on internal arrangements and their effectiveness:

- Section 2 describes the content and scope of force policy documents dealing with domestic violence.
- Section 3 discusses the role of specialist domestic violence officers, including how their scope differs between forces.
- Section 4 deals with the different organisational models adopted by forces in response to domestic violence and presents the views of interviewees as to their effectiveness.
- Section 5 looks at the recording and accessing of information on domestic violence incidents.
- Section 6 concerns the use of statistics and performance indicators to monitor the quality of the domestic violence response.
- Section 7 looks at training issues.
- Section 8 draws conclusions from the study findings.
- Section 9 presents a series of recommendations for consideration by the Home Office, HMIC, force headquarters and divisional commanders.

Terminology

Terms used to describe the major geographical and administrative subdivisions within police forces vary greatly, e.g. 'basic command units', 'divisions' and 'areas'. In the interests of consistency, this report refers throughout to divisions.

The term 'operational officer' is used to denote those nominated by their force to discuss the day-to-day approach to policing domestic violence. Most were specialists in dealing with domestic violence. In this report we have called these specialists domestic violence officers (DVOs), even though these words were not always included in their job title. Where appropriate, the report distinguishes the responses of DVOs from those of general operational officers.

2. Police policies on domestic violence

Policy statements play an important role in ensuring coherence of approach by different units within the force to domestic violence, particularly in respect of when cases should be referred to specialist officers. This section examines:

- the extent to which policy statements have been introduced by police forces;
- their content; and
- the extent of variations which exist between these documents.

The definition of domestic violence

In 1993 the Home Affairs Committee defined domestic violence as "any form of physical, sexual or emotional abuse which takes place within the context of a close relationship. In most cases, the relationship will be between partners (married, cohabiting, or otherwise) or ex-partners". Domestic violence is not a legally-defined offence and the police are not currently required to identify separately domestic violence incidents in their statistical returns to the Home Office.

Scottish HMIC (1997) has recommended that a standard definition be adopted which, for the most part, reflects the 1993 HAC definition, but also includes the requirement to maintain separate records on domestic violence incidents.[3]

The majority of definitions of domestic violence adopted by forces were based on that used by the Home Affairs Committee. However, variations did occur. The key ones included:

- relationships described: 10 forces (24%) specified that the definition applied irrespective of the genders of the offender or victim;
- behaviour defined: a few forces had adopted a relatively narrow definition of behaviour focusing on physical violence; and
- the range of offences recorded as domestic violence: some forces included damage to property.

Research has shown domestic violence to be an ongoing crime which persists over time and has stressed the importance of identifying repeat incidents. Only nine forces, however, referred to repeat victimisation in their policies and only one included a working definition of repeat victimisation.

Policies did not always make the link between domestic violence, rates of violent crime and homicide. Eight force policies (19%) contained information about the response to domestic violence involving ethnic minorities.

[3] *"For police recording purposes domestic violence is any form of physical, sexual or emotional abuse which takes place within the context of a close relationship between adults. In most cases the relationship will be between partners who are married, cohabiting or separated. Records will be maintained to differentiate between non-sexual crimes of violence, sexual offences and other crimes (such as breach of the peace, threats and vandalism) and abuse which does not amount to crime. Each record will also show the extent of repeat victimisation, and will be updated to show arrest/detention, report for summons/warrant, and any other outcome." HMIC for Scotland (1997).*

Policy documents

38 forces (90%) had a domestic violence policy document. Thirty five of these also had established written aims and priorities. Of the four forces with no policy document, these aims and priorities were set out in other documents produced by the force.

There were deficiencies in the configuration control of policy documents: most policies were dated 1996 or 1997, but four were between two and six years old and 14 were undated. Quality control procedures such as recording the date and issue number on every page, prescribed distribution and regular updating were not in place in the majority of forces. Policies in 26 forces (62%) were under review or being amended, particularly in light of legislative changes in the Protection from Harassment Act and Part IV of the Family Law Act. Several forces produced a version of their policy for publication, often in consultation with other members of their multi-agency domestic violence forum.

Wide variation was identified in the scope and content of domestic violence policy statements examined. No common structure was identified, nor was a standard checklist of matters addressed.[4] A typical policy document included information on:

- a definition of domestic violence;
- the implications of domestic violence; and
- guidance about the various components of the police response.

Reflecting the emphasis in Home Office Circular 60/90 on the use and value of powers of arrest, 40 (95%) forces also specifically mentioned the need for positive action and the presumption of arrest.

Responsibility for implementation of domestic violence policy is shared across a range of police functions. This was recognised to a limited extent in force policies, as illustrated in Figure 1.

4 *In the United States, efforts are being made to produce a model policy on domestic violence, initially at the state level and then nationally, to ensure the delivery of 'uniform and consistent services' e.g. Maryland Network Against Domestic Violence, 1997.*

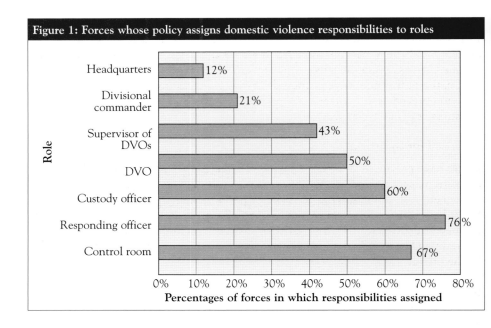

Figure 1: Forces whose policy assigns domestic violence responsibilities to roles

Domestic incidents involving police officers

The involvement of police officers or police support staff in domestic incidents, either as offenders or victims, was of concern to DVOs. Each of the five fieldwork forces had dealt with such incidents. Nationally, only one force policy referred specifically to domestic incidents involving officers as perpetrators. DVOs said that they would welcome guidance on complaints of this type and appropriate disciplinary procedures. Such guidelines would need to include:

- standard procedures for notification of senior officers when an alleged offence by a police officer has been reported;
- investigation procedures, e.g. some divisions assigned a DVO and investigator from elsewhere in the force if one of their own officers was involved;
- a clear message from Chief Constables to the police service and the public that domestic violence from officers would not be tolerated, and
- security provisions to ensure the integrity of any investigations and the privacy of the complainant.[5]

One commander said that it was an issue "rife with examples of surprisingly bad policing".

[5] For example, one DV office had installed security locks after an officer was found going through records trying to find his wife's address.

3. The role of the specialist domestic violence officer

This section looks in greater detail at key features of the specialist domestic violence officer role. Forces have, in the past, been recommended to employ officers who have a special responsibility for handling domestic violence offences. (Home Office Circular 60/1990). Even where forces have chosen to have specialist DVOs, the nature and scope of their duties vary. The section also examines selection procedures, the relationship between DVOs and their line managers and the stress associated with the job.

The need for specialists

Forces have previously been encouraged to set up 'dedicated' units specialising in domestic violence (Home Office Circular 60/1990). This message was reinforced in subsequent research findings (Grace, 1995). Nevertheless, six (14%) of the 42 forces had no officers specialising in domestic violence and a further 18 (43%) did not have a dedicated unit. In seven forces with a specialist unit, officers had other duties in addition to domestic violence. The majority of forces (86%) were found by the present study to have specialist DVOs.

Several forces without DVOs were considering the need for specialists. The increasing need to have a focal point for inter-agency work and for someone able to advise victims and other officers in respect of new legislation were particular pressures. Notwithstanding these pressures, one force said that it had rejected the appointment of DVOs on the basis that it would undermine the role of the patrol officer responding to domestic incidents and become an excuse to pass on problems which responding officers should properly address themselves. Many DVOs supported these concerns, arguing that they were often overloaded and that the nature of their work was not understood by colleagues who used them as a 'dumping ground'. The emphasis on working with victims sometimes branded DVOs as 'glorified social workers' and because the domestic violence response was not seen as a key factor in the force's overall performance, it had a low priority when assigning resources.

Profile of domestic violence officers

Of the 42 forces surveyed:

- 36 had appointed officers with special responsibility for domestic violence, an increase of almost 100% since Grace's 1995 study.

Of these 36:

- 18 DVOs were based in a domestic violence unit. In seven of these, officers had

other duties in addition to domestic violence, and
● 18 DVOs were not based in a dedicated unit.

Little pattern was evident in the numbers of specialist DVOs operating within any one force. The number of households served by a single DVO ranged from 2,000 to 286,000. Even forces within the same 'family' (grouping together those with similar characteristics) differed dramatically in the number of households per DVO. In nine forces (25%) the number of DVO staff had been decided by headquarters while in the others the decision had been devolved to divisions. Policy interviewees revealed that only five forces had attempted to match DVO staffing levels to demand.

In 12 forces, a third of those with DVOs, all were women, while in all but two of the remaining forces, women DVOs outnumbered their male colleagues. Nine forces had DVOs of ethnic minority background.

Nature and scope of the DVO role

Of the 71 DVOs interviewed, 65 (92%) were employed to deal with domestic violence incidents on a full-time basis.

For 37 DVOs (52%) domestic violence was their only responsibility. The duties of 16 of the other 34 DVOs included child protection, while the remaining 18 DVOs also had responsibilities in areas such as victim support, missing persons, community liaison and racial incidents. Eleven of the DVOs with other duties spent less than a quarter of their time on domestic violence duties. Even DVOs who had no duties other than domestic violence were sometimes seconded to other tasks. One in three of all DVOs said they felt under pressure to undertake other duties at the expense of their domestic violence work.

Job description

The domestic violence tasks that DVOs undertook varied widely between and sometimes even within forces. Sixty-two (87%) of the DVOs interviewed had a written job description but 34 (55% of the 62) of these said it was not an accurate reflection of what they did.

Figure 2 shows the range of activities undertaken by DVOs and the extent to which they occurred.

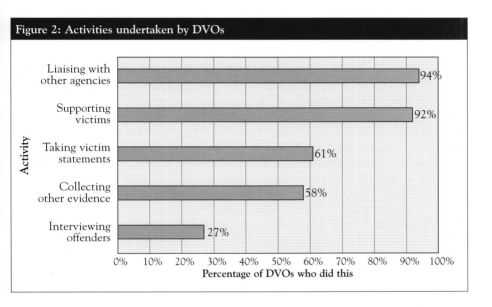

Figure 2: Activities undertaken by DVOs

In some instances the job description was in direct conflict with the service provided. As one officer commented, "we're told not to counsel but that's exactly what we do". This disparity between job description and practice contributed to a feeling expressed by many DVOs that senior officers understood little about the nature of their role. It also meant that the service provided often lacked focus or predictability and this in turn made it hard to monitor or co-ordinate.

In addition to attending meetings of their local domestic violence forum, DVOs spent much of their time liaising with other agencies. This was seen as important for increasing understanding of the police role and encouraging the commitment of agency resources to victims. In some areas DVOs felt that too much of the burden for promoting local initiatives fell on them. In one location visited during fieldwork, an attempt had been made to separate out those aspects of the job which required a police officer's involvement, with a civilian employee carrying out some of the telephone victim support and inter-agency work.

Administrative tasks also encroached on the time available to perform general functions. Thirty eight percent of DVOs claimed they spent more than half their time on administration. In particular, they quoted trawling command and control systems for missed cases, 'chasing' patrol officers for referral forms which had not been submitted and updating their own records. Forty-two DVOs (59%) said that administrative duties constrained their ability to provide an effective domestic violence response.

Some DVOs did not initiate contact with victims. For others the approach made to victims was ad hoc. The majority gave priority to repeat victims and those who had suffered serious assaults. Views differed as to whether letters should be sent after the first reported incident or whether a letter was ever an appropriate form of contact, as it might be opened by the offender. When DVOs were under particular pressure, making contact with victims sometimes assumed a lower priority.

The investigative role

Bridgeman and Hobbs (1997) argued that the work of the DVO should be integrated with other aspects of the response to domestic violence, involving detection, crime prevention and provision for victims "working together to one end".

In 16 forces (38% of those surveyed), at least one DVO interviewed acted as officer in charge of the investigation and interviewed offenders in more serious domestic violence cases.

The benefits were seen to be:

● more prosecutions;
● fewer cases being withdrawn by victims after the complaint was made; and
● a more positive status within the force for the DVO role.

One commander considered that it was more effective to place investigation and support in the same unit; an added benefit was that "intelligence flows more quickly into the mainstream".

However, most DVOs described themselves as playing no part in any investigation following the report of an incident. Only two line managers said they sought investigative skills when selecting candidates for the DVO role.

Thirteen DVOs (18%) were detectives although not all had received formal CID training. Only seven interviewees with policy responsibility (17%) thought that DVOs needed to be detectives, but 17 (41%) thought they should have more of an investigative role. However, they pointed out the resource implications because most

DVOs had difficulty in keeping up with the volume of work they already had. One quarter of the 52 DVOs who did not interview alleged offenders wished to do so. Not all DVOs were convinced of the benefits of involvement in investigations. Several were concerned that a conflict of interest would be created between investigation and victim support. Problems in liasing with investigating officers were reported by 30 (36%) of DVOs. This was particularly the case with CID officers who were sometimes unaware of the DVO role. One force had avoided these problems, while successfully achieving convictions, by having two kinds of DVO:

- an investigator who worked force-wide targeting serious repeat offenders, and
- others assigned to divisions who concentrated on working with victims.

This approach was thought to have been more successful in achieving convictions. Interviewees noted that child protection officers had become increasingly involved in the interviewing of offenders and thought that the development of the investigative role of DVOs should be formally evaluated.

Stress associated with the DVO role

Working directly with victims of crime is acknowledged to be stressful. The findings from this research reinforces this view. Several DVOs interviewed in the course of the study had had an extended absence due to stress and some nominated for interview were unavailable for this reason. Forces visited during fieldwork were only just beginning to monitor sick leave for DVOs. Interviewees suggested that rates of overtime should also be monitored as an indicator of overload.

Previous Home Office research recommended that 'ideally' two DVOs should work together (Grace, 1995). A few DVOs were assisted by a civilian employee or by another officer on attachment for a period of months. However, only 12 DVOs (17%) said that someone else undertook their domestic violence duties in their absence. Most felt a great sense of frustration and thought that too much of the burden of implementing force policy on domestic violence had fallen on them. One commented, "we all do our own thing in this position. Nobody would have a clue if I was doing nothing. As it is, I'm tearing my hair out."

Those DVOs who worked alone, with little or no cover for their absence, reported an increased sense of isolation and frustration. For example, one DVO working on her own pointed out, "In most police work, we work in pairs. Here, if I've got a tough job on, only I know about it." The often distressing nature of the work, a perceived lack of senior level commitment to dealing with domestic violence incidents, and a general suspicion of counselling services were also mentioned as contributory factors to this sense of isolation.

Only three (4%) of the 71 DVOs interviewed said unreservedly that domestic violence work was valued within their force. This lack of a sense of value was thought to contribute to the frustration and stress experienced by DVOs, as the following quotes illustrate:

"There is no credibility in dealing with domestic violence as far as my colleagues are concerned... the uniformed officers just don't want to get involved";

"The work we do is undervalued and nobody listens to us. As PCs, we have no clout";

"I talk at divisional meetings to inspector rank and below to raise awareness of domestic violence. I still get comments like *didn't you used to be a policeman?*".

While it was not expected that senior officers would necessarily have an in-depth knowledge of the day-to-day duties of the DVO, it was felt that they should at least be strongly committed to dealing with domestic violence incidents. There was some scepticism about the degree to which this occurred. One DVO observed that, "the Chief Constable's policy sounds great but it just isn't happening in practice". Another felt that, "the people who develop policy ignore the importance of the attitude of senior ranks. Nothing will change without their commitment."

Forty-eight DVOs (68%) said they had access to the force's counselling service, and a further 11 (16%) had access to a special support service. Perhaps as a result of this, only 20 (28%) felt that targeted counselling was needed for those in the DVO role. Nevertheless, many DVOs referred to the fact that the stigma associated with seeking counselling still persisted in police culture and many believed that a request for counselling might adversely affect their subsequent careers. One suggested solution was to make attendance at counselling sessions mandatory. This was being implemented in seven (10%) forces.

Fifty-three DVOs (75%) said they had the opportunity to exchange ideas with other DVOs within the force and 22 (31%) were in communication with DVOs in other forces. Fifty-nine (83%) thought that such contacts were, or would be, valuable.

Selection of DVOs

Managers described the requirements of the DVO role as including:

- inter-personal skills (empathy, compassion and being a good listener);
- communication skills; and

- the ability to work in a multi-agency setting.

DVOs had to be able to:

- work unsupervised and under pressure;
- prioritise;
- cope with stress, the frustrations of the role and grief-ridden work; and
- challenge the system.

Managers variously described desirable DVO characteristics as including being self-motivated; open-minded yet strong-minded; and flexible. It was important that they had a good health record without long absences for illness.

The emphasis on inter-personal skills may be linked to the perceived low status of domestic violence work within the force. The qualities identified as needed by DVOs all involved direct work with victims. Similar emphasis was not placed on understanding of civil and criminal legislation and the relationship between the two. Similarly, no manager mentioned the need for DVOs to have training skills as a trainer even though this accounted for a significant proportion of some DVOs' time. One in three of the DVOs interviewed had previously worked in child protection. However, child protection experience was considered important in selecting DVOs by only two line managers.

Managers and DVOs said that there could be problems in persuading candidates to come forward for selection and one in three line managers said they had difficulty in finding staff of the right calibre to become DVOs. Most forces followed the usual police procedure of advertising DVO posts and selecting applicants through interview boards. Despite the fact that two-thirds of line managers were actively involved in the selection process, some DVOs complained that members of interview boards often lacked an understanding of their function.

Relationship between DVOs and their line managers

The majority of DVOs and line managers identified problems with line management arrangements. Of the 40 line managers interviewed, 24 (60%) had a written job description of their domestic violence responsibilities but only 15 (38%) thought that it was an accurate picture of their actual duties. Sixteen (40%) had received training in domestic violence. Although over half of those questioned felt adequately supported by their own line managers in respect of their domestic violence role, a considerable number thought there was no clear management structure or interest for upward reporting of problems on this issue.

All but one of the line managers were responsible for other functions as well as domestic violence and for 23 (58%) the other functions included child protection which, it was universally accepted, needed to be given priority. Twelve line managers (30%) said they were called upon to resolve conflicts between the demands of domestic violence and other duties. Only 13 line managers (33%) said that they had sufficient time to carry out their domestic violence management responsibilities.

DVOs also voiced reservations about line management arrangements. Only 29 (41%) felt that the support they received from their line manager was adequate. Common complaints were:

- insufficient contact with managers who were often based in a different location;
- lack of management understanding of the domestic violence role; and
- failure to monitor caseloads, overtime and the amount of administrative work.

Many DVOs said that their line managers did not back them up in applications for resources, such as personal computers, which were becoming increasingly necessary to perform the role efficiently and effectively. One pointed out that she was expected to send letters to victims but did not have access to a word-processor. In another force the updating of a computerised cardbox system had been abandoned because of lack of administrative support.

The lack of clear lines of management responsibility for domestic violence led some DVOs who had little contact with line managers to take their problems directly to members of the command team. This generates its own problems: one sergeant commented, "I find myself being sidelined when then this happens but members of this unit are experts in their field and I am not trained".

Line management strategies

Table 1 shows the range of ways in which line managers in 36 forces were monitoring the performance of DVOs.

Table 1: DVO monitoring techniques used by line managers	
Technique	**Number who used (%)**
Through the appraisal mechanism	13 (36%)
Direct observation of DVOs at work	9 (25%)
Dip-sampling paperwork produced by DVOs	4 (11%)
No monitoring undertaken	4 (11%)
Systematic monitoring undertaken [1]	3 (8%)
Holding regular meetings with staff	2 (6%)
Using repeat victimisation figures	1 (3%)
Total	**36 (100%)**

[1] Of the three respondents who adopted a systematic approach, one talked of personal performance indicators, one referred to personal development plans relating to monthly performance indicators set for each division, while the third used performance and development reviews centred on 90-day plans which included performance targets.

Management support

The success of a specialist response was seen to depend more on the quality of management than on where the function lies within the organisation. It was felt that managers needed to:

- be involved in and committed to delivering a quality domestic violence response;
- be willing to fight for an adequate share of limited resources;
- be prepared to support their staff in resolving problems at the interface with other police functions; and
- be underpinned by commitment up the chain of command to the highest levels within the force.

These commitments should then be manifest in policy, training and performance monitoring, including a headquarters responsibility to monitor variations in performance throughout the force area. Without such commitment, the specialist function can become marginalised and isolated. This impacts operational effectiveness, lowers morale and results in a low status for the specialist DVO role in the eyes of fellow officers.

The majority of DVOs spoke of their need for a higher level of interest and support from managers. This was particularly important when they reported the poor practice of patrol officers, custody officers or control room staff.

To deal with the difficulties caused by lack of management involvement and sometimes geographical separation from managers, many DVOs had developed 'coping strategies' and alternative sources of support within and outside the force. Lack of supervision sometimes led to patterns of working that were not reflected in DVOs' job descriptions. This made managing and monitoring their work even more difficult which in turn increased their sense of isolation, thereby perpetuating the problems.

4. Force organisational structures

The research identified many different organisational approaches to domestic violence. This section examines the range of structures, their relative effectiveness, and the respective responsibilities of headquarters and divisions. The discussion draws on interviewees' perceptions of the domestic violence structure chosen by their force, their assessment of the problems encountered and suggestions for improvement. Organisational structures relating to domestic violence are compared with those relating to child protection.

Deployment of specialist officers

The location of domestic violence units and specialist DVOs within the force structure varied. This in part reflected recent organisational changes in the police service such as the introduction of local policing plans, moves towards sector policing and the Crime and Disorder Act 1998 with its focus on partnerships with local authorities. The cumulative effect of these changes has been to emphasise the devolution of management and budgetary responsibility to divisional and sub-divisional levels. Tension between central and local control often meant that there was no obvious or consistent 'home' for DVOs within force structures:

- 17 forces (47% of those with specialists) had DVOs located on divisions;
- 16 forces (44% of those with specialists) divided DVOs between headquarters and divisions; and
- three forces had DVO positions filled exclusively by headquarters personnel.

DVOs were not always deployed in a consistent way within forces, sometimes because of differing approaches among local authority areas. DVOs and DVO managers were sometimes stationed in different locations. Divisions within forces had occasionally decided to locate DVOs in different departments. As one DVO commented, "I'm in a uniform support role at the moment within Crime and Partnership. The post is shifting to come within the CID allocation, even though I'm not involved in investigations, but my line manager will still be in Crime and Partnership."

Organisational comparisons with child protection

It is useful to compare the organisational response to child protection and domestic violence because of the overlap between such incidents. Figure 3 shows the extent to which CID had responsibility for both policy and operations in these areas.

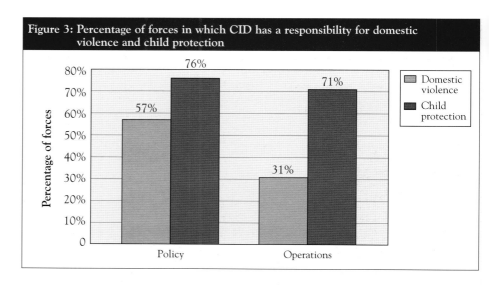

Figure 3: Percentage of forces in which CID has a responsibility for domestic violence and child protection

[6] "CPUs provide a consistent force endorsement of the inter-agency approach to child protection... the need for specialised facilities and training, and also for routine liaison with local authorities, has meant that centralisation has been the main option considered".
(Morgan, McCulloch and Burrows, 1995)

Also, in contrast to domestic violence, forces were more likely to retain central responsibility for the management of child protection.[6]

This study highlighted a number of issues to be contemplated by forces considering whether to link child protection work with domestic violence responsibilities. It confirmed the advantages and disadvantages identified by previous research of placing DVOs and child protection officers together organisationally (Grace, 1995). Although information sharing improved, problems were reported due to the higher priority given to child protection work.

Thirty-five DVOs (49% of the 71 interviewed) were managed by a supervisor who was also responsible for child protection. Line managers who supervised child protection were less likely to feel they had enough time to carry out their domestic violence responsibilities compared with other line managers. DVOs who had other duties were more likely to feel under pressure to take on work other than domestic violence if their line managers also managed child protection.

Perceptions of effectiveness

Perceptions varied widely amongst policy makers, line managers and operational officers as to the effectiveness of force organisational structures and the ability to deliver in practice the aims set out in policy statements. These differences are illustrated in Figure 4.

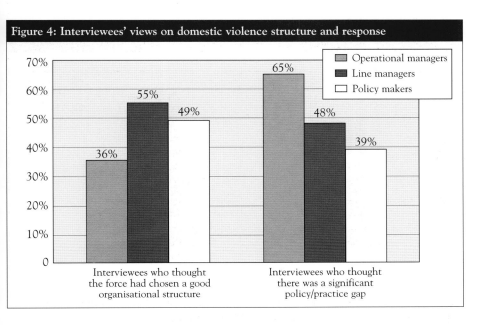

Figure 4: Interviewees' views on domestic violence structure and response

Legend:
- Operational managers
- Line managers
- Policy makers

Interviewees who thought the force had chosen a good organisational structure: 36%, 55%, 49%

Interviewees who thought there was a significant policy/practice gap: 65%, 48%, 39%

Structural problems

There was no correlation between the type of structure chosen by the force and its perceived effectiveness. Irrespective of the type of force structure in which they served, many interviewees described a management vacuum in which lines of accountability for the domestic violence response were blurred or did not exist. Operational officers were least convinced on the appropriateness of the structures in place. Two forces with DVOs were unable to nominate anyone in a line management position to be interviewed. Managers with whom interviews were conducted acknowledged doing little or no supervision, for example, "The DVU really runs itself."

Confusion between the management responsibilities of headquarters and divisional personnel further compounded problems. In one force, a headquarters inspector said, "I *act* as the DVOs' line manager but a sergeant on division *is* their line manager". The detective sergeant in question acknowledged, "the inspector at headquarters knows more about what they do but he is not their boss".

Those who felt that their force had not selected the right structure were asked to describe the problems it presented and to suggest improvements. Officers at all levels spoke of the need to integrate the domestic violence response with mainstream policing and to move away from the view that it was 'second class crime' if it was treated as crime at all. However, many thought that their force's organisational structure prevented such integration by marginalising those responsible for the domestic violence response. The feeling of isolation felt by many DVOs was apparent in comments such as, "I have no-one to take problems to" and "no-one in this force owns domestic violence".

Although most force policies referred to the need for a consistent level of response across the force to victims of domestic violence, over 60% of policy interviewees acknowledged that differences existed. For example: "the force approach is fragmented and controlled by division"; "the front-line approach varies, because divisional managers are inconsistent"; and "the domestic violence staff are divisional so the response varies. They've lost their way." Inconsistency of approach was mostly attributed to differences in attitude and commitment of individual divisional commanders. Only one interviewee said the variation in response reflected differences in local need.

There was a degree of scepticism about the commitment of headquarters to dealing with problems in the service delivery at a local level. One officer commented, "Headquarters is a eunuch without the wherewithal or will to do more than give broad guidance, but this means that divisions are having to re-invent the wheel. When personnel move across divisions, they find that roles and functions vary widely."

Another took the view that the pendulum had swung too far in the direction of devolution: "Some of the agencies we deal with cross divisional boundaries, and they find themselves dealing with different policies. Headquarters devolution has gone too far; the genie is out of the bottle."

Others felt that some inconsistency was unavoidable: "Much of the time we don't apply a force-wide policy. If you are in partnership with your local authorities, you have to pay attention to them. In this division we have to tailor our response to two authorities whose approach is very different."

The majority of interviewees at all force levels wanted to see an increased role for headquarters. Specific requests were for headquarters to:

● provide more direction;
● monitor domestic violence; and
● manage DVOs.

Some command team members and managers expressed frustration at headquarters' failure to provide guidance. For instance, "We have asked headquarters to help [with crime analysis] but they have just said to do whatever we need." One was even more outspoken: "Under devolution, the force no longer speaks with one voice on domestic violence. Headquarters should decide on the road and the minimum speed to move forward. As it is, we're all going in different directions."

Precise strategies for achieving consistency were unclear. Whilst some policy officers met DVOs on a regular basis, the DVOs' line managers were not always given the opportunity to meet together across divisions. Only six policy officers undertook active monitoring of some kind, usually through scrutiny of forms or statistical returns. Others were even more vague as to their approach, which they described as "influencing autonomous district commanders", "raising awareness with other agencies", and "stepping in where difficulties arise".

Organisational structures: best practice

Whilst no single organisational structure emerged from the research as superior to all others, DVOs identified a number of factors which were considered to benefit operational effectiveness:

- a strong headquarters role in setting policy and monitoring practice;
- separate line management of DVOs and child protection officers where this is necessary to ensure that domestic violence work is not subordinated to child protection;
- a vertical management structure extending to the highest levels within the force;
- the location of DVOs and child protection officers in the same or adjoining offices to facilitate the sharing of information;
- location of the DVO manager on the same site as the DVOs;
- domestic violence training for the DVO manager;
- opportunities for exchanging ideas with other DVOs within the force and externally;
- DVOs working in pairs for support and back up;
- monitoring of stress indicators such as turnover, sickness and hours of working; and
- administrative support and computerised record-keeping for DVOs.

Key factors concerning the location of DVOs included co-location with child protection officers and ease of access to operational officers and detectives. Many DVOs favoured being located in a police station but a minority felt that work with victims was facilitated by being located elsewhere.

5. Information management

[7] These factors were emphasised in Home Office Circular 60/1990.

Key factors in an effective response to domestic violence include comprehensive record-keeping on domestic incidents and ease of information retrieval.[7] However, police information systems have developed in a fragmented way and many forces are only in the early stages of developing a more integrated approach. As a result, although police records often contain information about previous incidents at the same address or involving the same family, this is not always readily accessible to responding officers. This section highlights the lack of a systematic approach to information needs and information sharing practices.

Command and control systems

Responding appropriately

Command and control systems have the potential to hold, provide and relay a variety of useful information, for example:

- coding of domestic incidents;
- information about previous domestic incidents at an address, which can subsequently be passed to responding officers;
- referral of domestic incidents to DVOs; and
- information about children.

Emergency calls are dealt with by police command and control rooms. Their primary function is to serve the public and allocate police resources through 'demand management'. Calls are given a priority allocation linked to a target response time. Although control room staff acknowledged that domestic incidents should generally be given a high priority, in some of the forces visited, DVOs were concerned that a small proportion of calls were disposed of by telephone operators in ways contrary to force policy. In one of the worst examples, a caller from a hospital casualty unit had been told that a domestic incident "was not a police matter".

There was also some evidence that those responding to calls had not followed them up in an appropriate way. For example, an operator following up a failed '999' call accepted the reassurance of a man at the other end of the phone that everything was all right. The operator closed the incident as 'phone resolution' on the control room computer system. It later emerged that when the operator had made the follow-up call, the aggressor was standing with a foot on the woman's throat.

[8] Most DVOs work day shifts and are not on duty or call out at nights or weekends.

In some instances, calls assigned a low level response (aiming to have an officer attend the address within four hours) were allocated for action by the DVO, even though no DVO would be on duty within the stipulated response time.[8]

Call coding

In addition to assessing response priorities, control room operators classify calls by assigning opening codes which broadly designate the type of incident. Additional descriptive codes are then attached when the incident has been dealt with and closed. All but one force have in place an incident logging system with a designated code for domestic incidents. However, seven forces reported that they coded for domestic 'violence' only. Forces varied as to whether the system required a single closing code to be selected or allowed a combination of closing codes to be used.

Control room supervisors acknowledged the difficulty of achieving a reliable and consistent level of accurate coding by the large number of officers and civilian control room staff. A number of underlying problems were identified. Although incidents were occasionally miscoded, a potentially greater problem was that while the assigned code might be accurate, it might not necessarily include the code designating a domestic incident. Serious assaults against the person were particularly problematic in this respect. The performance of control room operators is assessed in terms of the timeliness of the police response, not the accuracy or completeness of coding. As a result, code assignment was of low level importance. Many operators were unlikely to be aware of their force's definition of domestic violence. As one supervisor said, "the incident is only what the operator perceives it to be. This is not a system for producing statistics". Without operator awareness of the definition of domestic violence it is impossible to ensure that an accurate response is recorded.

Another problem lies in the dependence of control room staff on operational officers for information. One observed, "if we had to chase officers for accurate results so as to code correctly we'd never get anything else done". The information given may be misleading or patrol officers may ask the operator not to code an incident as 'domestic' in order to avoid having to complete the paperwork required for referrals to DVOs. These practices were also acknowledged by some of the patrol officers interviewed.

Incident tagging

In addition to coding, some control rooms tagged certain incidents on the computer system to designate them for the attention of DVOs. Where systems permitted tagging, control room supervisors felt the tag was a useful feature as it provided a method for highlighting domestic incidents which was independent of code assignment. Nevertheless, tagging suffers from the same reliability problems that afflict the coding procedure.

Trawling

DVOs reported that they could not rely on coding or tagging procedures to identify all domestic incident calls received by the control room. 'Trawling' involves DVOs going through records of calls received by the control room in an attempt to identify domestic incidents of which they should have been made aware. As they felt that they could rely neither on coding nor tagging procedures to identify all of them, 47 DVOs (66%) conducted their own trawls of control room records to identify domestic incidents. Although universally regarded by DVOs as a time-consuming exercise, trawling is likely to be a necessary part of the DVO role until coding and tagging are performed accurately and reliably. The range of the trawl varied from a review of all incidents in a particular time period to a narrower scrutiny of assaults, arrests and abandoned '999' calls. One control room supervisor said that after a DVO complained about the proportion of missed cases, he instituted a check and found that only 50% were being tagged correctly.

Information for patrol officers responding to a domestic incident

Historical information

Responding patrol officers were said to be given historical information about previous incidents at the address by 35 forces (83% of those in the survey). This was seen as particularly important in relation to officer safety. As one officer said, "You can't risk assess without this information". However, patrol officers noted this information was not routinely passed on in all cases: "Operators don't always tell you if there is any history so I always ask." Others said that they sometimes found out that the control room computer held previous history only after they returned to the station and were completing their own paperwork: "Too often, we're going in blind".

When an incident was reported, control rooms in different forces differed in the ways they could access information about previous incidents at the location.[9] In general, the easier the process for accessing this information, the more likely operators were to pass it on. If operators had to access a second screen for the information, they sometimes failed to check it. The most straightforward systems brought up historical information on the screen automatically and required the operator to assess whether it was relevant to the current incident; if the operator thought it was, the history was linked to the current incident. This automatic linking was reported by DVOs to be very helpful when printed out on reports. Command and control systems could give historical information about previous calls to the address (though not always to

[9] *Operators were usually expected to pass historical information to patrol officers, although the control room supervisor in one force said this was not required because the target for operator response time was so tight.*

the precise street number) over a period ranging from the previous 30 days to over a year.

Markers

The use of domestic violence 'markers' varied widely. Markers were used by DVOs to flag up addresses on the command and control system where:

- alarms had been installed or a priority need for information to be passed on existed;
- there was concern about repeat victimisation; or
- there was a perceived need for positive action.

The number of available markers varied and criteria for their use were rarely written down. Some DVOs reported being restricted to about five or six markers, while others used around 40. Some forces felt that the more markers there were on the system, the more likely they would be ignored or down-played. Practice relating to their use lacked consistency; DVOs often had no way of knowing if information associated with the marker was passed on to patrol officers, but sometimes they became aware during follow-ups that the officers had not been told. Sometimes markers were deleted from the system without reference to the DVO. Limitations on the use of markers and questions about their effectiveness made frequent review important, but this rarely formed part of the responsibilities of either the DVO manager or the control room supervisor.

In most computer systems, a few lines of history could be attached to the marker. However, in one force, operators seeing the marker were expected to refer to a manual binder with information to be passed on to the responding officers. The supervisor and operators were unaware of the meaning of the marker or the need to refer to the binder.

Other information

Other information which could be of importance to responding officers included the existence of injunctions, powers of arrest, bail conditions or procedures under the Protection from Harassment Act 1997. These could be mentioned briefly in markers or history. Such information was usually available in the control room on paper records only. The process by which copies of injunctions reached the control room and the way in which they were filed and maintained was erratic, with operators often relying on the caller to tell them whether an injunction was in force.

Referrals to DVOs by officers attending domestic incidents

Sixty five (92%) of the DVOs interviewed by telephone received information about domestic incidents from patrol officers, usually on a specially designed form. Estimates of the proportion of incidents for which a form was produced varied among forces from over 90% to fewer than 50%. DVOs identified incidents for which responding officers had failed to make a referral by trawling coded incidents on the command and control system, or by cross-checking with incidents tagged to DVOs by the control room.

It was a standard requirement that referrals be made to the DVO before the end of the patrol officer's shift. Speed was crucial as the effectiveness of any follow-up by the DVO diminished as time since the incident increased. However, the information recorded on forms varied between forces and sometimes among divisions within a force. Sometimes officers forgot to obtain information required by the form such as the names and dates of birth of children. One force supplied officers with a small plastic card with a reminder of the categories of information required; others encouraged officers to carry the form in patrol cars. Further delays could be caused by the shift system; for example, if day-time DVOs had to 'chase' officers on night duty, delays of days or even weeks could occur before information was obtained.

Even where an incident had not been recorded as a crime or was closed as no further action, information contained in report forms was found to be useful by DVOs. On occasions, however, this information was not passed on as officers did not see why it might be relevant for the DVO to log it. Training by DVOs was thought by some to have improved both the quality and timeliness of form completion by responding officers, although these messages needed to be reinforced by managers. Other DVOs felt that there was little they could do to improve the performance of patrol officers. They complained about the lack of support from supervising officers: "We have to work with the uniforms again so we can't make waves...there is no point in complaining to sergeants or inspectors about poor completion – they're just the same."

Such problems were acknowledged by supervisors themselves. Even where procedures for dealing with problems existed, they were rarely used. For example, one inspector described a procedure for DVOs to bring 'problem' forms to him if an officer failed to respond to requests for information, so that the inspector could take this up with the shift supervisor. He admitted that he had never actually intervened on a DVO's behalf in this way.

Accessibility and quality of information in domestic incident records

In addition to command and control systems, DVOs kept their own records of incidents. Figure 5 compares the frequency with which information on a number of key areas was available from both of these sources. It was evident that DVO records held more information.

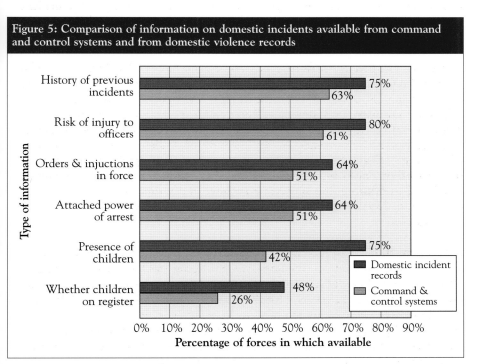

Figure 5: Comparison of information on domestic incidents available from command and control systems and from domestic violence records

Specialist officers in 20 forces (48%) kept at least some domestic incident records on computer, although in eight of these records held in other divisions were not computerised. Access to computerised DVO records was available force-wide in only 10 forces. Only one control room visited during fieldwork could access directly domestic incident records held on computer. Delays were also common where command and control systems were not automatically updated with historical data. Occasionally, records were weeks in arrears. The timeliness of data input was not a performance measure routinely reviewed by managers.

The marginalisation of domestic violence within some forces had caused it to be left behind in the movement towards intelligence-led policing. DVOs and their managers were frustrated that the information they held was not considered as a useful police resource. Examples included detectives in homicide cases failing to contact DVOs, even though domestic violence records held information about the family. Commanders complained that there was little or no input from domestic violence records into crime intelligence. One said, "DVOs here are policing a population with a lot of police contact. They could be a hub for problem-solving and intelligence, but the extent to which they feed into our information systems is minimal."

Communicating information about children

Domestic violence is a feature of many of the child protection cases with the worst outcomes, yet professionals often give little attention to children's exposure to high levels of violence (Farmer and Owen, 1995). This highlights the need for good communication between child protection officers and DVOs, and also with social services departments.

The current study revealed variations in the way forces responded to the presence of children in households where a domestic incident took place. The main differences were in:

- the use of markers on the command and control system to identify addresses where children were on the child protection register;
- the actions taken by patrol officers when children were in the house at a domestic incident, and the information recorded;
- the criteria for communicating information about an incident to social services;
- the responsibility for passing on such information (sometimes DVOs preferred this to be done by police child protection officers); and
- the existence of an integrated child protection and domestic violence index.

A more accurate measure of risk can be provided if the whole family situation is considered, but few forces in this study had been able to integrate indices. Thirty six DVOs (43%) described themselves as co-located with child protection officers, but few actually shared an integrated index. Exchanging information involved checking and updating two sets of records. Where DVOs and child protection officers were in different police premises, communication for the purpose of checking and updating records was much more difficult. As one child protection officer commented, "When we are on the phone here or out of the office, we are not available to answer queries from DVOs".

Some forces used a flag on the command and control system to notify officers responding to domestic incidents that a child at the address was on the child protection register (see Figure 5). The information flagged could also be accessed by DVOs and child protection officers.

Reasons given for not using a child protection flag were:

- the number of children whose names were held on the child protection register;
- the need for the system to be updated if a family moved (relying on information from social services); or
- the number of names removed from the child protection register.

One force had conducted a survey in part of its area to check the number of times officers were called to addresses where a child was on the register. The force policy officer described the level of call-out revealed by the survey as "staggering – much higher than either we or social services had been aware of". Over a 17-month period, the police logged an average of five visits to each register address: one address had been visited 61 times. One third of all these calls concerned domestic violence. The survey was considered so valuable that it was extended force-wide. The findings underscored the liaison responsibilities of DVOs and resulted in an increased demand for them to attend case conferences.

There were inconsistencies in relation to where information was stored and what information was available in different locations. For example, information about children on the register in one force was held on the local intelligence system but not on command and control. The child protection officer interviewed mistakenly believed the local intelligence system could be accessed by command and control and that the information was therefore available to patrol officers. The local intelligence officer felt that the information should have been on the command and control system.

A further problem identified by DVOs was the lack of adequate communication between themselves and social services. There appeared to be no standard criteria across forces as to when information should be passed to social services about a child in a household where a domestic incident had been reported. Practices in place include:

- automatic referral to social services of all incidents where there was a child at the address;
- referral of 'selected' incidents only;

- referral only if it was thought that children might be harmed physically;
- no referral if the children were asleep when the incident occurred;
- informing social services of a single serious incident or three less serious incidents in a short period of time;
- asking the police child protection unit to refer where there is a second incident; and
- leaving the decision to child protection officers on whether to refer to social services.

Some DVOs had arranged to share information with health visitors and education welfare officers, although the passing on of information to social services and other agencies was seldom the subject of written inter-agency agreements.

Many senior officers expressed concern about uneven practice across the force on this issue, a problem exacerbated by the subdivision of old local authority areas and the creation of new unitary authorities. Many forces dealt with eight or more social services departments. A command team member who felt strongly that all incidents with children should be passed on said it was up to individual social services departments to decide how to manage the information, and that DVOs "should not let the volume floor them". Another said that social services and Area Child Protection Committees needed to have a proper audit trail of what was happening with these referrals and pointed out that DVOs are not in a position to carry out a risk assessment as they do not have the full picture of what is happening to a child. Senior managers were also concerned that officers invited to attend 'children in need'[10] rather than 'child protection' case discussions would have difficulty in passing on information about families because of data protection concerns.

[10] *Multi-agency committees to address 'children in need' were part of children's services plans introduced by Local Authority Circular LAC (92) 18. The 1995 Department of Health report 'Child Protection: Messages from Research' had suggested a shift of focus in which more children would be identified as being 'in need' and fewer as requiring 'protection'.*

6. Monitoring

A key factor in the success of any domestic violence response is the adequacy of arrangements to monitor both the level of demand and the quality of the service being delivered. The information that monitoring provides is a prerequisite for effective performance management. If monitoring is not in place, the message conveyed is one that domestic violence is of low importance, reinforcing negative attitudes to this work which may exist within forces.

The study looked at forces' monitoring arrangements in relation to the levels and patterns of domestic violence offending within the force area and to the quality of the response provided. In both cases there was little evidence of a systematic approach to monitoring or effective mechanisms for using the information that emerged to improve performance. Forces are encouraged to take positive action through arresting domestic violence offenders (Home Office Circular 60/1990). Sixty six per cent of forces measured the proportion of incidents which resulted in an arrest, compared with 95% of forces which emphasised the presumption of arrest in their policies.

Monitoring the level and pattern of domestic violence offending

Information on the extent of domestic violence offending can inform decisions about staffing levels and deployment. The data are also useful in detecting changes in reported offending patterns and assessing the effectiveness of the force's response. However, the interpretation of the figures needs care, especially as incidents are often dealt with in a manner that assigns them a low profile within the criminal justice system. For instance, common assault was not a recordable offence at the time of the study and neither breach of the peace nor breaching bail conditions is a crime.

Thirty-eight (93%) of the 41 policy interviewees indicated that their force collected some statistics relating to domestic violence offending. Table 2 shows which statistics were collected and how many forces collected them.

Table 2: Statistics collected on incidence of domestic violence	
Type of information	Number that collect (%)
Total number of incidents	38 (93%)
Repeat victimisation	24 (59%)
Complaints against offenders from injured parties [1]	16 (39%)
Complaints that are subsequently withdrawn	12 (29%)
Other factors [2]	5 (12%)

(1) Many reports to the police of domestic violence incidents are not made by victims but by others such as neighbours. In such cases, the victim may decline to make a complaint against the alleged abuser. This explains why the number of incidents and the number of complaints against offenders are separate entries in this table.

(2) Other statistics collected include: the number of incidents involving violence; the number of incidents involving drink or drugs; the number of incidents in which children were in the house; and the ethnic origin, age and gender of both victim and offender.

Monitoring the quality of the domestic violence response

Performance indicators and statistics

Forces are recommended to make comprehensive record-keeping a central feature of force policy;[11] the commitment of senior officers is thought to be more likely if they have a stake in performance outcomes. Table 3 shows the statistics that are collected and the number of forces which collect them.

[11] *Home Office Circular 60/1990.*

Table 3: Statistics collected on response to domestic violence	
Type of information	Number that collect (%)
Arrests	27 (66%)
Number of incidents giving rise to a crime report	24 (59%)
Referrals to outside agencies	14 (34%)
Cautions	13 (32%)
Charges	13 (32%)
Refused charges	10 (24%)
Police bail with conditions	5 (12%)
Other factors [1]	8 (20%)

(1) Other response statistics included: domestic violence forms completed each month; domestic violence incidents giving rise to police child protection proceedings; offenders detained in police custody; offenders who are bound over; statements taken; meetings with victims; incidents giving rise to a prosecution and the outcome; court appearances; and incidents in which no further action was taken.

Statistics are useful as performance indicators only when the information they contain is used to assess and improve the effectiveness of the force's response. Policy interviewees in the 38 forces who collected statistics were asked how they used the data collected. Only 30 were able to reply:

- 6 (20%) responded definitively that the data were used to generate statistical reports which were then used in reviewing performance;
- 11 (37%) gave a vague response, for instance "We're just starting to use them," "they're used in discussions" or, "They feed in to our monthly statistics but domestic violence does not appear as a separate category;" and
- 13 (43% of the 30 who responded) said they did nothing with the data.

Some DVOs prepared an annual report containing statistical tables. These could be useful in raising and resolving specific problems. For example, one report included the number of attempts to contact the DVO by phone which encountered an engaged signal. The force call-logging analyst recommended diversion of such calls to a second extension with an answering machine.

Twenty-six policy interviewees (63%) indicated that their force's domestic violence response was subject to an internal review mechanism. Measuring the quality of service to victims has been shown to provide a more rounded picture of police effectiveness (Bridgeman and Hobbs, 1997). However, only six (15%) forces had carried out victim satisfaction surveys.

Managers in some of the fieldwork areas found performance indicators relating to first-line response to be most useful, for instance, the proportion of incidents that resulted in an arrest. The presumption of arrest was mentioned in 95% of force policies; this key performance measure was used by 27 forces (66%). There was general agreement that indicators were particularly valuable when comparing the performance of different areas within the force. One manager stressed the need for exception reports to highlight anomalous performance in a particular area. Another manager in headquarters had used statistics to compare the performance of areas with differing domestic violence staffing levels.

Comparative data can also be of value in assessing the performance of DVOs. There was evidence that some forces had failed to appreciate this. For example, in one force in which divisions were being further sub-divided into sectors, DVOs had only been asked to provide each sector separately with statistics relating to their performance, but had not been asked for this information on a comparative basis.

The research revealed that no force monitored its domestic violence response in totality, that is by looking at all the individual components – control room, patrol officers, custody sergeants and DVOs – and the interfaces between them. However, many of the problems occur at these interfaces, such as:

- control room officers not providing responding patrol officers with historical information about incidents and not coding incidents as domestic violence;
- patrol officers not referring cases to DVOs; and
- custody officers not charging offenders who had been arrested.

Accountability

The Police and Magistrates' Courts Act 1994 introduced the concept of accountability through the publication of policing plans. As well as forming an agreement between the chief officer and the police authority, policing plans tell the public what services and standards they can expect.[12] They can also aid performance monitoring. Inclusion of an objective on domestic violence is an effective way of making the issue central to the force as a whole. However, many senior officers acknowledged that domestic violence was either not included in force-wide or local policing plans, or was mentioned without the attachment of specific targets or performance indicators.

This was attributed to a pervasive view that forces are not held accountable nationally or locally for their domestic violence performance. There are no national key objectives or key policing priorities relating specifically to domestic violence. A detective inspector in headquarters in one area said statistics were submitted to area command teams and it was stressed to them that domestic violence accounts for 18% of violent crime. The officer felt that teams had difficulty in making this connection as domestic violence statistics were not part of area targets which relate to car theft, burglary and violent crime overall. These were linked in turn to budgetary incentives which were the dominant concern.

Commanders also noted that domestic violence did not form part of periodic reviews conducted by assistant chief constables. Commanders suggested that domestic violence indicators should be developed in collaboration with those who had operational responsibility, included in the force plan and then made mandatory for divisions using, as one put it, "a mutually agreed model with minimum parameters".

One area commander's local plan included a low-level objective relating to domestic violence (to hold a number of meetings with social services). However,

[12] *Crime and Disorder Act 1998 crime reduction strategies will provide further opportunities for whole force support for a particular policing responsibility.*

responsibility for these meetings had been assigned to a community affairs liaison inspector, even though that officer had no responsibility for the domestic violence function. The commander admitted that no one with direct responsibility for domestic violence had taken part in the development of the plan. This failure to involve those responsible for the domestic violence response in the development of policing plans was repeated in other forces.

Data reliability and use of IT

Although this study did not examine systematically arrangements for data collection, some facts relevant to data reliability emerged during the course of interviews and fieldwork. As well as distorting performance figures, poor data can directly impact on staffing levels. In one force a proposal to cut a domestic violence position had been based on numbers which did not include all domestic incidents in the system or referrals to the DVO from external sources.

Concerns were voiced about the forms used by responding officers to report incidents of domestic violence to DVOs. These forms are also a key source of statistical data on domestic violence. (The diligence with which these forms were completed was discussed in the previous section.) In one force visited during fieldwork, the system for providing reports, including those generated by officers responding to domestic violence, had recently been computerised. Paradoxically, this had resulted in a reduction in the number of domestic violence reports being completed and a consequent under-counting of the total number of incidents, perhaps because crime reports were seen as having higher priority.

Well-designed IT systems can help in improving the response to domestic violence. If computerised information is available force-wide, the database can be searched across the force area for names of offenders and victims who have moved. However, most of the computerised card-box systems maintained by DVOs were stand-alone and contained information on local incidents only, and DVOs in different divisions of the same force often used different data collection software. The value of a standard force-wide system was not always recognised. One headquarters inspector with domestic violence responsibility had tried and failed to get funding for a standard system; another manager commented, "To get a standard database across the force would have meant going before users' committees for two years". If the commander wanted domestic violence statistics, it was quicker to get a system funded on division and designed by the local performance manager. Other problems with these systems were millennium incompatibility and limitations on the size of database that could be accommodated.

DVOs commonly had backlogs of forms awaiting data entry to computer – sometimes of weeks or even months. These backlogs not only degraded the accuracy of domestic violence statistics but also hampered support to repeat victims because of the incompleteness of available historical information. Further record-keeping problems arose for DVOs who had no one to cover for them when they were not available. The lack of adequate cover was referred to by over 80% of DVOs interviewed. In one force, a domestic violence officer was seconded to a murder inquiry and, as a result, her division failed to provide monthly statistics for almost a year.

Problems were also encountered in relation to other force computer systems. Many custody systems include a field which allows domestic violence to be recorded but DVOs reported that this was rarely filled in and so the statistics produced differed from those based on domestic violence forms.

Repeat victimisation

It is estimated that 90% of domestic violence to women involves systematic and often escalating violent behaviour. Repeat victimisation figures are useful in monitoring performance and focusing the work of DVOs. Despite the fact that many senior officers felt that the ability to demonstrate a reduction in repeat victimisation was an important indicator of success,[13] 41% of policy interviewees said that their force did not monitor the level of repeat victimisation.

A few DVOs were trying to target repeat victimisation systematically: as repeat incidents were identified, the DVO would carry out a series of tasks following a specific pattern, for instance a letter to the victim followed by a telephone call and finally a home visit. Such a structured response allowed the effectiveness of different interventions to be monitored and forms a basis for evaluating the success of the work of the DVO.[14]

Even in forces committed to reducing repeat victimisation, problems had been encountered in developing a simple way to identify and count the number of repeats. Some forces restricted attention to incidents of a similar type within a given period. Others did not use a specific time interval but instead checked through all records that had been computerised. There was widespread concern that computer systems could not adequately identify repeat incidents. One of the forces that produced statistics on repeat victimisation had been forced to rely on the crime reporting system for data. The DVOs' computer records could not produce this information.

[13] The Home Office's key performance indicator for repeat victimisation defines it as occurring when the same person or place suffers from more than one incident over a period of time. The report 'Preventing Repeat Victimisation: the police officers' guide' suggests that a 12 month rolling period should be used, as "anything less may hide relevant crimes and anything more may become unmanageable" (Bridgeman and Hobbs, 1997). This report gives a 'worked example' demonstrating how to calculate the extent of repeat victimisation.

[14] For a detailed example of a staged response, see Bridgeman and Hobbs, 1997 at pp.17-18. This sets out three levels of intervention for victims and perpetrators in the Killingbeck domestic violence project.

In order to understand the pattern of domestic violence locally and also to measure the effects of any intervention, three measures are relevant: the number of incidents (incidence); the number of incidents of repeat victimisation (concentration); and the number of victims (prevalence). The forthcoming Killingbeck report discusses how these measures should be considered in combination (Hanmer, Griffiths and Jerwood, forthcoming). If, for example, following a preventive initiative, the number of incidents remained constant this could be because there had been no effect. An alternative and desirable reason for the lack of change in incidence would be that repeat victimisation had fallen but that more women were reporting attacks, shown by an increase in prevalence. Ultimately, when 'saturation' is reached (because there is not a limitless supply of women requiring police attendance) one would expect to see the overall numbers of incidents reduce if repeat victimisation continued to be effectively prevented.

7. Training

Training on domestic violence is important for all ranks, not only to give officers the necessary skills but also in order to challenge outmoded attitudes and to ensure appropriate force policy is implemented. This section examines training provision in general and the special arrangements for those with responsibility for domestic violence. It also looks at the involvement of DVOs in training delivery. Arrangements for training trainers and involvement in external training programmes are discussed. In general, training provision was patchy, even for specialists, and forces appeared to lack a strategy for delivering training to senior personnel and others with a key role in the force's response to domestic violence.

General training provision on domestic violence

Thirty-five forces (83%) said that they provided in-house domestic violence training to officers other than specialists. In 17 forces, the only training given on domestic violence was to probationers as part of their initial general training and induction. In a further 17 forces the target audience was probationers and constables. Only one force trained a wider group. Most of the constables interviewed during the fieldwork said they had not received in-force domestic violence training, even though they worked in forces which claimed to provide such training.

Where in-house training was given, it was heavily dependent on the contribution of DVOs. Forty six (65%) delivered training to other officers. They emphasised the need to treat training on domestic violence as a rolling programme, to reinforce good practice and attitudes to 'positive action' which otherwise fell away over time. Updates were necessary because of new legislation and the development of local initiatives. Sometimes offers to provide training for various police groups had, as one DVO put it, "fallen on deaf ears". Some DVOs had tried to target control room staff, custody officers, detectives and shift sergeants, but with varying degrees of success. It was thought to be particularly difficult to get senior officers to attend training but where this had happened, it raised the profile of domestic violence work generally throughout the force.

Some training methods were felt to be more successful than others. Training approaches which had been helpful included playing tapes of domestic violence calls, reviewing the record of police responses to incidents that had eventually resulted in homicide and discussing policing strategies to break the cycle of repeat victimisation. Input to tutor constables, who act as mentors to probationers, was thought to be important.

A number of forces were in the process of introducing some form of attachment for constables to introduce them to the work of DVOs. The length of time involved varied, with the longest lasting several months. It was felt that longer assignments allowed DVOs and their managers to screen potential future candidates for the position. All such attachments helped spread awareness of domestic violence issues. One force had developed detailed objectives for a two-week attachment for probationers. It asked them to complete questionnaires assessing their knowledge at the beginning and end of the attachment. These involved asking the probationer to respond to a number of hypothetical scenarios.

Training for those with special responsibility for domestic violence

Twenty nine managers (69%) and 55 operational officers (66%) described domestic violence training as deficient in some respect. 30 forces (71%) considered that additional police training was required as a result of new legislative provisions in Part IV of the Family Law Act 1996 and the Protection from Harassment Act 1997.

Twenty forces (56%) reported that officers with special responsibility for domestic violence received training for their role. Fourteen forces (70%) said that training was delivered through in-house courses, mostly lasting between three and five days, although two forces provided a 10-day course. However, only 28 operational officers (33%) and 16 line managers (38%) had received such training. Interviewees in 15 of the forces which reported providing courses said they had not received any specialist training.

Evidence suggests that some of the most successful training on child protection and domestic violence is delivered jointly by trainers representing both specialisms (Hendry, 1998). However, DVOs and child protection officers in fieldwork forces said that they rarely received training together.

Training the trainers

DVOs said that training skills were crucial to their job although often they were not taken into account in staff appraisal. Although a few DVOs delivered courses with the help of force trainers, many of them conducted training on their own and much of this work was undertaken on the DVO's initiative. It often took a significant amount of their time. One DVO said, "The amount involved is always grossly underestimated – I spend a third of my time on training". The lack of involvement from official trainers was due in part to the many competing priorities for police training, but one DVO described this as unfortunate, as "training needs to be owned by the training department".

A one-week 'training for domestic violence trainers' course for all DVOs, which they had found very valuable, has been conducted by one force in the study. In the divisions where their offers to provide training had been accepted, these DVOs had seen an improvement in the police response, in turn reflected in positive letters from victims and solicitors. However, the majority of DVOs in other forces said they had received little or no training as trainers themselves.

Training other organisations

Most DVOs were involved in external training. Some were systematically working their way through groups represented on the domestic violence forum and this consumed a significant proportion of time. Targeting primary health care teams – health visitors, GPs and midwives – was felt to increase the number of referrals to DVOs.

8. Conclusions

This section draws together conclusions from the report presented under the relevant section headings. These conclusions form the basis for the recommendations made in section 9.

Police policies on domestic violence

- The lack of a nationally agreed definition of domestic violence is a major obstacle to assessing police performance. Because of this, statistics cannot be directly compared. Agreeing a national definition is essential if reliable national statistics of reported recorded incidents are to be produced.

- To ensure that domestic violence policy is both relevant and communicated effectively, it is important that controls relating to the production and updating of policy documents are in place.

- It was clear from the study that complaints of domestic violence, either against or by police officers, require specified procedures which allow them to be investigated in confidence and without bias.

Force organisational structures

- Forces in the survey had used different organisational models in designing their domestic violence response and some had adopted different models within the same force.

- No single structure emerged as more or less problematic than any of the others. The problems related less to the structure than to the status of domestic violence work within forces, the level of commitment of headquarters and divisional commanders, the clarity with which responsibilities were defined and the effectiveness of management arrangements.

- In many forces where responsibility for DVOs had been devolved to divisions, headquarters staff retained little or no managerial oversight for the force response or responsibility for inconsistencies in the performance of different divisions.

- The apparent lack of direction or oversight of domestic violence matters on the part of headquarters communicated itself down through the command structure resulting in a generally low status for domestic violence work.

- Arrangements for managing domestic violence work were often unclear with managerial commitment lacking and lines of accountability blurred.

- This led to domestic violence often being marginalised within the force. One consequence of this was that advantage was not taken of the information in domestic violence records to improve the quality of intelligence available more generally throughout the force.

The role of the specialist domestic violence officer

- DVOs provided a valuable resource which was not being used to the police service's full advantage. The position tended to be inadequately and inaccurately specified in force documentation and was not sufficiently integrated into mainstream policing. These problems contributed to poor monitoring of the role and to low awareness of its potential importance to other police functions. An underlying problem encountered by DVOs was the persistence of outdated attitudes to domestic violence including a perception that it did not constitute core police business.

- There was no standard model for the DVO role among forces in the study. A wide spectrum of activities were represented, including victim liaison and support, liaison with external agencies, training delivery within the force and externally, involvement with investigations and administration. Some DVOs had little or no direct contact with victims; others did little else. For those with responsibility for training and inter-agency liaison, or under pressure to perform administrative tasks, contact with victims often accounted for a relatively small proportion of their time.

- Most DVOs took no part in investigations. Those who worked closely with investigating officers described significant benefits to the prosecution process, although some DVOs were concerned that an investigative role might undermine their work with victims.

- Those performing the DVO role often felt marginalised and under-valued within the force. The low status of the role added to the stress already felt by DVOs because of their contact with victims. Reported stress levels were higher still for DVOs who worked alone.

- The feeling of isolation was compounded by managers who adopted a 'hands-off' approach. Few systematically monitored the performance of DVOs. Many managers were reluctant to press for more resources on behalf of DVOs or to get involved in resolving problems at the interface with other police functions. Few DVO managers were held accountable for how they carried out the task.

- Administration had become the dominant task for many DVOs who were therefore making little use of their years of experience and training in operational police work.

Information management

- The mechanisms for identifying domestic incidents appeared unreliable. Reports to DVOs from patrol officers and the coding or tagging of domestic incidents by control room operators both under-counted the true figures.

- Officers responding to incidents could not rely on the control room to tell them about information held on the command and control computer including previous incidents at the address and the 'markers' containing other relevant information.

- Information in manual records held in the control room, such as injunctions and Protection from Harassment Act orders, was seldom communicated to responding officers.

- Local domestic violence records held more detail than command and control systems. Much of this was directly relevant to officers responding to incidents and to police intelligence systems. However, even where a domestic violence database was held on computer, it was seldom accessible by the control room.

- DVOs spent excessive amounts of time seeking information on incidents which should have been provided to them routinely.

- Few forces had been able to integrate the information held on child protection and domestic violence databases, even though the same families often appeared on both. Most DVOs and officers responding to domestic incidents did not have ready access to information about whether children at an address were on the child protection register.

- DVOs in some areas were left to exercise their own judgement about whether to communicate with social workers about children in households where domestic incidents were reported. The criteria for passing on information were unclear and were rarely incorporated into written inter-agency agreements.

Monitoring

- Forces' monitoring arrangements in respect of domestic violence varied widely.

Apart from the total number of incidents, no other single statistic relating either to incidence or performance was collected by more than two out of three forces.

- Repeat victimisation, acknowledged as a key indicator in this field, was measured by only 59% of forces. Moreover, the term 'repeat victimisation' was interpreted in different ways. No standard time interval for repetitions was used.

- Few forces used the information contained in their statistics constructively and standards of performance monitoring were generally low. Most divisions received no data on how their performance compared with others within the force, although where this information was circulated it was considered to be of great value.

- No force had adopted a 'systemic' approach to monitoring their domestic violence response by looking at all the police functions involved and how effectively they worked together.

- The inadequacy of monitoring arrangements was linked to a pervasive view that domestic violence performance did not affect significantly a force's standing. There were no national key objectives or key policing priorities that referred specifically to domestic violence. There were few references to domestic violence in policing plans and little acknowledgement of the high proportion of violent crime that is domestic in origin.

- The low status of domestic violence work affected the reliability of data collection and the willingness to assign scarce IT resources for the collection of domestic violence statistics.

Training

- Despite the prominence of domestic violence in policy, forces generally did not have a coherent training strategy to ensure its effective implementation. Much of the training had been developed on an ad hoc basis.

- Only one force routinely provided training on domestic violence to ranks higher than constable.

- A minority of interviewees had received domestic violence training, even in forces which claimed to provide it, and the majority described training as deficient in some respect.

- Most forces thought that additional training would be required to address recent criminal and civil legislation.

- The burden of training, both within the force and externally, fell heavily on DVOs. Even though they saw their involvement in training as worthwhile, it was time-consuming and often took place at the expense of other domestic violence duties. Some said that their managers were unaware of the proportion of their time taken up by training within the force and to external groups.

- The DVOs' training contribution was often provided without assistance or back-up from force trainers. Many DVOs had received little or no training as trainers themselves.

9. Recommendations

This section sets out a number of recommendations arising from the study findings. These are aimed at assisting forces in developing an appropriate and effective organisational response to domestic violence. Although it was initially thought that recommendations would be aimed at forces themselves, it emerged during the study that certain improvements would require Home Office action. For this reason, the recommendations are grouped according to the different audiences to which they are addressed, namely the Home Office, force headquarters and divisional commanders. A final recommendation relates to aspects of forces' domestic violence response which should be included in HMIC inspections.

Police policies on domestic violence

Home Office

It would be beneficial if a definition of domestic violence were developed which meets the criteria set out in the report by the Scottish HMIC. Forces should be encouraged to adopt this definition in their domestic violence policy and to use it in providing statistical reports to the Home Office. A clear message on the importance of monitoring repeat victimisation should also be given to forces. This should include re-stating the recommendation of a 12 month rolling period over which such monitoring should be carried out. These steps would greatly improve the ability to monitor force performance.

Guidance for forces should be developed on the content of domestic violence policy documents. The guidance should include procedures to be followed in the case of a complaint by or against a police officer in relation to a domestic incident.

Force headquarters

Policy documents should carry a date, an issue number and a distribution list. There should also be a specified period between reviews.

Guidance should be developed for divisions relating to the handling of complaints of domestic violence involving a police officer. This should ensure that such complaints are dealt with by senior officers and with the necessary sensitivity.

The role of the specialist domestic violence officer

Home Office

Research should be conducted to evaluate the benefits and drawbacks of different models for the DVO role, in particular the use of DVOs in an investigative capacity, and the contribution of civilian support personnel.

Force headquarters

Clear priorities should be established for the tasks DVOs are required to perform.

Divisional commanders

Divisions should develop job descriptions for the DVO role which reflect the priorities set by headquarters. The time spent by DVOs on each task should be monitored as part of performance management and the scope of the role reviewed regularly in the light of the results. Line management responsibilities at a divisional level should also be clarified.

Force organisational structures

Force headquarters

Individual force headquarters should restate their commitment to the quality and consistency across divisions of the forces' response to domestic violence. They should develop a statement of how that commitment will be delivered. This is likely to include:

- developing meaningful performance indicators and targets relating to domestic violence;
- requiring divisions to provide headquarters with statistical data on a regular basis to allow these indicators to be calculated;
- undertaking to provide divisions with comparative performance data and taking appropriate action where performance falls below an acceptable standard;
- monitoring stress indicators associated with the DVO role such as turnover, working hours and sickness rates, and ensuring that stress counselling is available if needed;
- standardising aspects of the response across divisions, for instance by introducing a standard domestic violence format for reporting; and
- identifying and promulgating best practice and developing pilot projects.

Forces might usefully review the relationship between child protection and domestic violence, focusing on issues of management, co-location, training and information sharing.

Divisional commanders

Divisions should consider establishing and documenting lines of accountability for their domestic violence response. The responsibilities of all those in the chain of command should be set out in writing and used as the basis of formal monitoring and progress reporting.

The role of the DVO should be more clearly integrated into the force structure by clarifying its interface with other police functions involved in responding to domestic violence. Standards of performance in relation to domestic violence should be specified for each of these functions and formal mechanisms established to allow the resolution of operational conflicts that arise.

Information management

Home Office

The Home Office, together with the Department of Health, should provide guidance to police forces and social services departments concerning the communication of information about children in households in which domestic violence incidents are reported. Criteria for passing on information should be incorporated into written inter-agency agreements which should address data protection concerns.

Force headquarters

Periodic monitoring of the transmission to officers of historical information and information contained in markers should be seen as part of any assessment of the domestic violence response. There should also be monitoring of the accuracy with which domestic violence incidents are coded, and the effectiveness of tagging specific incidents for the attention of DVOs.

Divisional commanders

Divisions should review practice relating to the following aspects of information management:

- DVOs' use of markers on the command and control system;
- access to information held on DVOs' systems; and
- forwarding of domestic incident reports to DVOs.

Monitoring

Home Office

A schedule of statistics for forces should be developed to facilitate performance monitoring at a national level.

HMIC

During its inspections, it would be beneficial if HMIC continued to assess the quality of forces' arrangements in respect of domestic violence.

Force headquarters

Force headquarters should consider specifying core parameters relating to domestic violence performance which divisions must measure and report on a regular basis. Based on the returns, headquarters could then produce and distribute statistical reports comparing the performance of divisions as measured by the core parameters. The requirement to produce statistics could be reflected in policing plans. The list of core parameters is likely to include:

- number of incidents;
- number of incidents of repeat victimisation;
- number of victims;
- number of arrests;
- number of incidents that give rise to a crime report; and
- proportion of violent crime that is domestic in origin.

Divisional commanders

Divisions should audit their data collection and referral mechanisms to ensure that the statistics produced accurately reflect the work being undertaken.

Training

Force headquarters

A comprehensive force training strategy on domestic violence for all officers should be developed, addressing awareness of its nature, procedural knowledge and the high proportion of violent crime that is domestic in origin. It should pay attention to officers with a key role to play in delivery of force policy but who have been previously overlooked, including shift sergeants, control room staff and custody officers. The strategy should include senior officers whose commitment to the delivery of force policy is essential.

Training should be delivered as a rolling programme with regular refresher elements. Links should be made between training and deficiencies in practice revealed by monitoring and evaluation.

Force headquarters should ensure that DVOs who are required to conduct training do so with some back-up from force training specialists. They should also ensure that these DVOs receive training as trainers and that the amount of time involved is monitored.

References

Bridgeman, C and Hobbs, L (1997) *Preventing Repeat Victimisation: the police officers' guide.* Home Office Police Research Group.

Department of Health (1995) *Child Protection: Messages from Research.* HMSO.

Department of Health (1998) *Working Together to Safeguard Children: New Proposals for Inter-Agency Co-operation. Consultation Paper.* Department of Health.

Edwards, S (1986) *The Police Response to Domestic Violence in London.* Central London Polytechnic.

Farmer, E and Owen, H (1995) *Child Protection Practice: Private Risks and Public Remedies.* HMSO, London.

Grace, S (1995) *Policing Domestic Violence in the 1990s.* Home Office Research Study 139, Home Office Research and Planning Unit.

Hanmer, J, Griffiths, S and Jerwood D (forthcoming) *Arresting Evidence: Domestic Violence and Repeat Victimisation.* Home Office Policing and Reducing Crime Unit.

Hendry, E (1998) *Children and Domestic Violence: A Training Imperative.* Child Abuse Review Vol. 7: 129-134.

HM Inspectorate of Constabulary for Scotland (1997) *Hitting Home: A Report on the Police Response to Domestic Violence.* Scottish Office.

Maryland Network Against Domestic Violence (1997) *Model Domestic Violence Policy for the Maryland Law Enforcement Community. Fifth Draft.* Maryland Network Against Domestic Violence.

Morgan, J, McCulloch, L and Burrows, B (1995) *Central Specialist Squads: A Framework for Monitoring and Evaluation.* Home Office Police Research Group.

Morley, R and Mullender, A (1994) *Preventing Domestic Violence to Women.* Home Office Police Research Group.

Smith, L (1989) *Domestic Violence.* Home Office Research Study 107, Home Office Research and Planning Unit.

RECENT POLICE RESEARCH GROUP AND POLICING AND REDUCING CRIME UNIT PUBLICATIONS:

Police Research Group
Crime Detection and Prevention Series papers

88. **The Nature and Extent of Light Commercial Vehicle Theft.** Rick Brown and Julie Saliba. 1998.

89. **Police Anti-Drugs Strategies: Tackling Drugs Together Three Years On.** Tim Newburn and Joe Elliott. 1998.

90. **Repeat Victimisation: Taking Stock.** Ken Pease. 1998.

91. **Auditing Crime and Disorder: Guidance for local partnerships.** Michael Hough and Nick Tilley. 1998.

92. **New Heroin Outbreaks Amongst Young People in England and Wales.** Howard Parker, Catherine Bury and Roy Eggington. 1998.

Policing and Reducing Crime Unit
Police Research Series papers

93. **Brit Pop II: Problem-oriented policing in practice.** Adrian Leigh, Tim Read and Nick Tilley. 1998.

94. **Child Abuse: Training Investigating Officers.** Graham Davies, Emma Marshall and Noelle Robertson. 1998.

95. **Business as Usual: An Evaluation of the Small Business and Crime Initiative.** Nick Tilley and Matt Hopkins. 1998.

96. **Public Expectations and Perceptions of Policing.** Russell Bradley. 1998.

97. **Testing Performance Indicators for Local Anti-Drugs Strategies.** Mike Chatterton, Matthew Varley and Peter Langmead-Jones. 1998.

98. **Opportunity Makes the Thief.** Practical theory for crime prevention. Marcus Felson and Ronald V.Clarke. 1998.

99. **Sex offending against children: Understanding the risk.** Don Grubin. 1998.

Home Office
Research, Development and Statistics Directorate

WARD LOCK

FAMILY HEALTH GUIDE

BREAST CANCER
& BREAST CARE

WARD LOCK

FAMILY HEALTH GUIDE

BREAST CANCER
& BREAST CARE

CAROLYN FAULDER

IN ASSOCIATION WITH
BREAST CANCER CARE

WARD LOCK

Carolyn Faulder is a medical journalist who has also written numerous books on breast cancer. She is the Chairwoman of Breast Cancer Care.

A WARD LOCK BOOK

First published in the UK 1995
by Ward Lock
Wellington House
125 Strand
London
WC2R OBB

A Cassell Imprint

Distributed in the United States
by Sterling Publishing Co., Inc.
387 Park Avenue South, New York, NY 10016-8810

Distributed in Australia
by Capricorn Link (Australia) Pty Ltd
2/13 Carrington Road, Castle Hill, NSW 2154

A British Library Cataloguing in Publication Data block for this book may be obtained from the British Library.

ISBN 0 7063 7411 8
Designed by Lindsey Johns and typeset by The Design Revolution, Brighton
Printed and bound in Spain

Acknowledgements
The publishers would like to thank Breast Cancer Care for their help in producing this book, and for providing the photograph on page 73. Photographs on the following pages are reproduced by courtesy of Life File: 2 (Juliet Highet), 11 (Terence Waeland), 17 and 32 (Nicola Sutton), 20 (John Cox), 24 (Emma Lee), 25 (Keith Curtis), 26 (Flora Torrance), 29 (John McBain), 30 (Ray Ward). Others who have kindly supplied photographs are the North Downs Community Health NHS Trust: 34, 38, 42, 58; Melanie Friend: 70, 72; David Palmer: 68; Adrian Pope: 76.
Cover photograph: Paul Mattock.

Contents

Introduction

This is a short book about a major health care concern for women. Breast cancer, once a taboo subject, now frequently grabs the headlines and women are bombarded with distressing stories and often conflicting information. Attention has focused on the appalling 'breast cancer lottery' known to exist in this country whereby it is a matter of chance – where you live and what doctor you see – whether you get the best treatment or something less, ranging from inadequate or worse.

Professor Roger Blamey, a leading breast specialist in this country, recently said at a public meeting:

A woman who finds a breast lump may be seen in a specialist breast clinic the day after she consults her GP and receive all the diagnostic tests necessary at one visit. On the other hand she may be referred to a non-specialist general surgical clinic, have to wait weeks or even months for an appointment, be referred for a mammogram weeks later, be seen several times by junior staff who cannot make a decision, and finally receive an inappropriate operation for the removal of her lump. Everyone who works in breast disease will recognize these extremes.

Breast cancer kills some 15,000 women a year in the UK. We cannot allow this shocking situation to continue. Do not allow anyone to play the lottery with your life.

This book contains all the basic information you need to know about prevention, risk factors, diagnosis, treatments and aftercare for breast cancer. It details what is current best practice, based on the Macmillan ten minimum standards of care for breast cancer (see opposite). These were drawn up on the advice of more than 30 experts in breast cancer and they do not exceed anything stated in the Patient's Charter.

If you are not satisfied with the treatment you are being offered, say so immediately. Do not put up with anything less than the best. And if you really find it impossible to get the information and help you need, remember that you are always entitled to seek a second opinion.

Carolyn Faulder

Minimum standards of care for breast cancer

Every woman should have:

1 a prompt referral by a family doctor to a team specializing in the diagnosis and treatment of breast cancer, including a consultant from within the team;

2 a firm diagnosis within four weeks of being referred to a hospital by a family doctor;

3 the opportunity of a confirmed diagnosis before consenting to treatment, including surgery;

4 access to a specialist breast care nurse trained to give information and psychological support;

5 full information about types of surgery (including breast reconstruction where appropriate), and the role of medical treatments (for example, radiotherapy, chemotherapy, Tamoxifen);

6 a full explanation about the aims of the treatments proposed and their benefits and possible side effects;

7 as much time as she needs to consider treatment options;

8 a sensitive and complete breast prosthesis fitting service, where appropriate;

9 the opportunity to meet a former breast cancer patient who has been trained to offer support;

10 information on all support services available to patients with breast cancer and their families.

(*Source*: leaflet of Macmillan Breast Cancer Campaign 1994.)

Chapter one
Know your breasts

Breast awareness

Most girls in their teens feel self-conscious about their breasts, especially while they are developing and changing their appearance. Most women can probably remember a time in their life when they were concerned about their breasts. They might have felt that they were too big, too small, or the 'wrong' shape. As time goes on, however, most of us become able to accept our breasts the way they are and feel comfortable with them.

We look and are individuals in every way. Our faces are different and so are our breasts. For instance, it is quite usual to have one breast either slightly larger than the other or placed slightly higher on the chest wall.

Every woman should remain sensibly aware of her breasts throughout her lifetime. Breast awareness simply means knowing what is normal for you, and knowing what to do when 'normal' might have become 'abnormal'.

The developing breast

The human breast is a paired mammary gland which appears as a minute swelling in the six-week-old foetus.

At birth both sexes have an elementary internal system of large milk ducts, linked externally to two nipples, each surrounded by a small circle of deeper pink called the areola.

At puberty, usually some time after the age of 11, when a girl starts secreting oestrogen and progesterone, the hormones controlling sexual development and fertility, her breasts begin to swell, the nipples become more pronounced and sebaceous glands appear as small bumps on the areola. Internally the milk ducts start branching out into smaller ducts which end in tiny milk-producing glands. The milk glands are clustered in lobes embedded in fatty tissue and linked to the ducts which converge like the spokes of a wheel on to a central reservoir just behind the areola. This is where milk collects when a woman is breastfeeding.

During adolescence the lobes and ducts continue to grow. Fat and connective tissue accumulate around them, giving the young adult female breast its characteristically spherical firm shape. Breast tissue is attached to

8

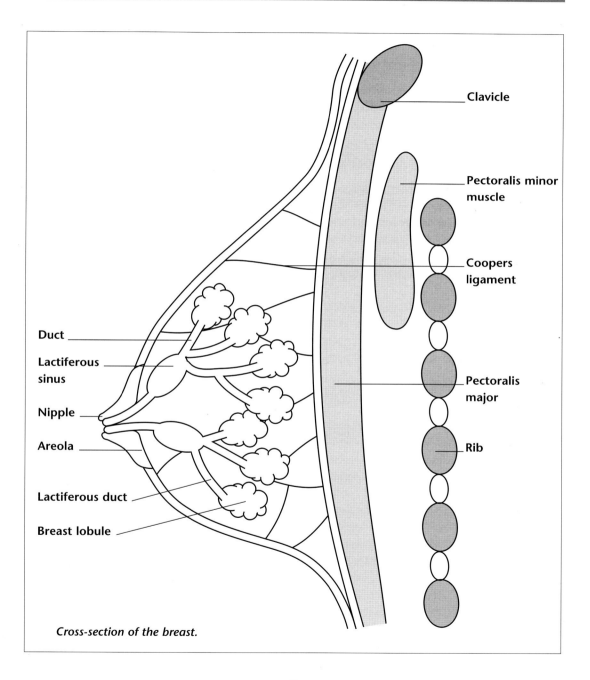

Cross-section of the breast.

Clavicle

Pectoralis minor muscle

Coopers ligament

Pectoralis major

Rib

Duct

Lactiferous sinus

Nipple

Areola

Lactiferous duct

Breast lobule

Know your breasts

the underlying pectoral (chest) muscles and the overlying skin by fine strands of fibrous tissue known as Cooper's ligaments.

Final breast size depends on how much fatty and fibrous tissue develops in an individual woman. The size of your breasts will not affect your ability to breastfeed since the internal mammary gland area behind the nipple is approximately the same size in all women.

Each breast is surrounded by lymph glands which have a two-way defence function. They act as a filter system to protect the breasts from harmful agents that may be circulating through the body. They also fight to prevent spread of disease from the breast into the rest of the body. Lymph glands are located in each armpit (axilla), above the collar bone and behind the central breast bone where the ribs meet.

The changing breast

A woman's breasts go through many normal changes over a lifetime. These occur mainly because her hormones are constantly fluctuating.

Every month, during the reproductive years, the breasts prepare for pregnancy and lactation. After ovulation, when the egg is shed from the ovary, the milk glands swell, frequently causing the breasts to become enlarged and tender. If the egg is not fertilized, the lining of the womb (endometrium) will be discarded during the monthly period and the breasts will return to their normal state.

Pregnancy has an immediate enlarging effect on the breasts as the milk glands prepare themselves for action. After giving birth, if the mother decides to breastfeed – good for her health as well as her baby's – the breasts will continue to produce milk for as long as they are stimulated. When breastfeeding stops, the breasts return to their normal size.

As a woman approaches her menopause, her breasts begin to change shape and texture. Internally the tissue becomes less dense and the ligaments lose their elasticity; externally the fact that her body is producing less oestrogen causes them to lose their former firm fullness. In old age the breasts shrink and grow smaller, or become pendulous if they were once large.

Although all these changes are normal and to be expected, many women do experience an exaggerated reaction to certain changes at some stage in their life. The severity varies. What may be tolerable for one woman can be either extremely painful or produce a disturbing symptom for another.

Whatever the problem, do not ignore it. It is always sensible to report any breast change immediately to your family doctor. You will not be wasting the doctor's time, nor are you being over anxious.

Hormone fluctuations are responsible for many normal changes in a woman's breasts, and pregnancy has an immediate enlarging effect.

Know your breasts

How to look for change

To be properly breast aware you must take care of your breasts, checking how they look and feel, in a non-obsessive way. From time to time, but no more than once a month, and preferably after your period when your breasts are soft, do a breast self-examination.

Examining your breasts

Start by taking a close look at your breasts in the mirror, arms hanging down. Then lift your arms slowly and turn from side to side, looking for any changes in the shape and size of your breasts. Look at them sideways as well.

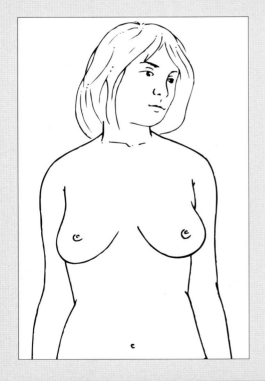 

Examining your breasts

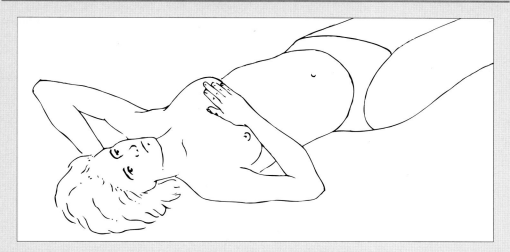

If you prefer to do a more thorough examination, follow the instructions below.

1 Lie down with one arm by your side. Bring the opposite arm across your chest, lay your hand flat on your breast and gently press it in a circular movement with the pads of your fingers, gradually moving centrally into the nipple area. Then repeat the same

exercise with the other breast.

2 Raise one arm above your head and do the same gentle pressing with your fingers underneath and around the breast and in the armpit. Repeat with the other breast.

Many women find that they can feel with more sensitivity by pressing all over their breasts with soapy hands and fingers when they are having a bath or a shower.

Changes to look for

Differences in size or shape between the breasts
- One breast has become smaller.
- One breast feels different – harder or tighter.
- One breast looks different – has changed shape or is facing in a different direction.

Differences between the nipples
- Either of the nipples turned in or pointing differently.
- Discharge of any kind (without squeezing the nipples).
- Rash or swelling on the nipple or the areola.

Know your breasts

Differences in skin texture on one or both breasts
- Any puckering, dimpling or obvious drawing-in.
- A rash.
- Thickening of the skin.
- 'Orange peel' skin.
- A visible lump or bulge.

Changes to feel for
Lumps, swelling or thickening
- A lump in either breast or armpit.
- A lumpy area or thickening anywhere in the breast.
- Enlarged glands under either armpit.
- Swelling of the upper arm.

Changes to note
Any pain, sense of discomfort, or a persistently painful area in either breast that feels different from premenstrual tenderness.

If you make a regular monthly habit of following this 'look-and-feel' routine, you will soon be very familiar with what is normal for you. And should there be a change, you will feel more confident about deciding whether it is just part of your monthly cycle or indicates another cause which may not be serious but could be helped by treatment.

Should you have any doubts at all, go and see your family doctor at once. Although the doctor may be fairly certain that you do not have a serious problem, he or she may want to refer you to a specialist in breast disorders because you may need treatment. At the hospital you may be given a mammogram (breast X-ray), ultrasound or other tests to enable the consultant to make a diagnosis.

Certain hormone treatments do sometimes provide some relief, but they can also cause unpleasant side effects. Breast specialists are all agreed that antibiotics and diuretics are useless for breast problems and should not be prescribed.

Take heart! More than nine times out of ten, breast problems are not caused by cancer. So what does cause them?

Some common breast disorders

Many women find at some time in their lives that their breasts are causing them anxiety. Perhaps you often have tender painful breasts, or your breasts may feel lumpy at different times in your menstrual cycle, or most of the time. You may suddenly be alarmed by an obvious change like a lump or a discharging nipple that seems to appear overnight.

All these vague but undeniably disturbing and sometimes painful symptoms have, in the past, been given a variety of confusing names under the umbrella term 'benign breast disease' which does not have a very reassuring ring about it. Doctors prefer now to be much more precise and careful in their terminology and classification of such disorders.

Breast pain (mastalgia)

Breast pain is probably the most common condition of all, experienced, it is estimated, by two out of three women at some time in their life. There are two types of breast pain:

● **Cyclical:** relating to your monthly period. Typically, the breasts feel heavy, swollen and tender for several days before each period.

● **Persistent/intermittent non-cyclical:** often described as a 'burning' or a 'drawing-in' sensation.

Keeping a pain chart, like the one illustrated below, for two or three months enables the doctor to determine which kind of breast pain you are suffering.

Continuing breast pain, whether cyclical or other, must always be investigated.

Pain chart

		M	T	W	T	F	S	S
0 = no pain								
1 = mild pain		0	1	0	0	2	0	0
2 = moderate pain	September	1	1	0	0	0	0	0
3 = severe pain		3	3	2^p	3^p	3^p	2^p	2^p
4 = very severe pain		1	1	0	0	0	0	0
P indicates the days of your period		1	1					

Self-help tips particularly for cyclical pain

● Ensure that you have a well-fitting supportive bra.

● Cut down on caffeine (tea, coffee, chocolate).

● Reduce your fat intake.

● If you are overweight, lose weight.

● Vitamin B6, vitamin E and oil of evening primrose have all proved effective for some women.

● Stop smoking if you are a smoker.

Know your breasts

Lumpy breasts

Women with naturally lumpy (nodular) breasts tend to be especially sensitive to monthly periods. Some lumps appear unexpectedly.

Fibroadenoma is a lump of fibrous, glandular breast tissue usually found in women aged under 35. It can be quite large and feels firm yet mobile. This type of benign (harmless) tumour is twice as common in black women as in white women and may appear in both breasts. It may have to be removed surgically if it causes discomfort.

Cysts are common in older women approaching the menopause. They are fluid-filled sacs which may feel soft or firm and can sometimes be quite painful, particularly before a period. Often there are multiple cysts in one or both breasts.

You should be checked by a consultant who can draw off the cyst fluid, using a syringe with a very fine needle, which allows the cyst to collapse. This simple procedure, called fine needle aspiration (FNA), can be done in an outpatient clinic without anaesthetic. A doctor may sometimes send the fluid away for laboratory analysis, but the prevailing medical opinion is that this is usually unnecessary. However, if the doctor finds it difficult to aspirate the cyst, producing little or no liquid, or perhaps some blood, which could suggest a solid lump, or the lump persists, further tests will be necessary, including a surgical biopsy (see Chapter four).

Cysts have a habit of returning in about one-third of women but they usually disappear soon after the menopause. Treatment remains the same. Recurrent cysts very slightly increase the risk of developing breast cancer.

Other common breast problems

Mammary duct ectasia is a condition which causes the milk ducts beneath the nipple and areola to dilate as they fill with fatty debris. This causes irritation of the nipple and a thick grey-green discharge; it may also retract the nipple. Although usually painless, it can become intermittently painful if neglected. Acute attacks can be successfully treated with antibiotics. Stopping smoking is most important.

Nipple discharge (yellow, milky or blood-stained) can have a variety of causes, usually non-cancerous. For instance, intraductal papillomas are small wartlike growths in the lining of a mammary duct which typically cause bleeding from the nipple. They usually occur in women in their late forties and can be removed surgically.

Flat or inverted nipples are common to many women, but always report any marked change of appearance such as the nipple 'pulling in'.

Mastitis is a breast infection which occurs usually in women who are breastfeeding. Bacteria enter through the nipple and the breast becomes inflamed, tender and painful. It is essential to treat this condition immediately, usually with warm compresses and antibiotics, so that an abscess does not develop and the woman can continue to breastfeed.

These and other changes mentioned earlier, like skin puckering, dimpling, a rash, or an alteration in the shape of one breast, should always be reported without delay to your doctor. Usually the solution will be relatively simple.

Giving up smoking is recommended whatever your state of health, but is especially important if you are suffering from mammary duct ecstasia.

Breast awareness is about understanding what is normal for you while at the same time being alert to problems that may appear. Unfortunately breast cancer is always a possibility, especially as you become older. British women have a one-in-twelve lifetime chance of developing this disease.

If you have some particular reason to be worried about developing breast cancer, perhaps because one or more members of your family have had breast cancer before their menopause, do let your doctor know. This is a sensible precaution and he or she may suggest referring you to a consultant for further examination, or to a genetic clinic where you can be given regular check-ups and counselling.

17

Chapter two

Who gets breast cancer?

Facts about breast cancer

Worldwide, breast cancer is the commonest female cancer, accounting for 18 per cent of all cancers contracted by women. There is, however, a significant geographical variation. Japanese and other Far Eastern women have six times less risk of developing breast cancer than Western women. A low-fat diet and a much later menarche (onset of periods) are two of the reasons given. Yet once Japanese women emigrate to Western countries – North America, for instance – or even if they adopt a Western lifestyle in Japan, the picture changes. Within two generations these women become as susceptible as their Western sisters. This indicates that environment is more important than genetic factors, but the precise elements cannot yet be pinpointed.

Breast cancer is a blanket term for about 20 different kinds of malignancy that can occur in the breast. The natural history of the disease – what causes it and how it develops – is still not well understood, so while we can theorize about high- and low-risk factors and the genetic element, two-thirds of the women who develop breast cancer do not fit into these high-risk categories. In our present state of knowledge we can do little more than speculate about possible environmental and lifestyle influences. It seems probable that in most cases breast cancer is a multifactorial disease: a variety of 'events' having a compound effect that ultimately results in disease.

In Britain we hold an unenviable record: we have one of the highest mortality rates from breast cancer in the world and we rank second only to the USA for incidence of the disease. However, the very latest figures show an encouraging downward trend particularly among younger women.

Hidden behind these bald statistics are

More facts about breast cancer in Britain today

- One in 12 women is at risk of developing breast cancer during their life.
- 30,000 women are diagnosed with breast cancer every year.
- 15,000 women die of breast cancer every year – 300 women every week.
- Breast cancer is the main cause of death in women aged between 34 and 55.

thousands of individual tragedies, repeated year after year. It is no exaggeration to state that breast cancer is rapidly assuming epidemic proportions and that doctors seem powerless to bring it under control, despite improvements in treatment and aftercare. This is something of an irony at a time when the mortality rates from childhood leukaemia and testicular cancer, to take just two examples of other cancers, have dropped dramatically – as a result of breakthroughs in treatment, not because of a reduced incidence. Breast cancer rates will improve only when women receive higher standards of treatment.

Risk factors

Age

Age is a significant risk factor. Before 30 you are unlikely to develop breast cancer, even if you have a history of producing benign lumps. All the same, nearly 500 cases a year are diagnosed in this age group, so you should always report any abnormal change in your breasts to your family doctor and ask to be referred to a specialist if you are still worried after examination. Do not accept the brush-off: 'You are too young for breast cancer.' Some women are not.

As you approach the menopause your risk increases; and thereafter, since more of us are living longer, we all become more vulnerable the closer we get to old age. Forty per cent of all breast cancers are discovered in women aged over 70, *but the tumour may not be a new one.* Breast cancer, like many other cancers, is a latent disease, often taking as long as 30 to 40 years to develop after the initial cause. We know this from the effects of two established causes:

● **Ionizing radiation** of the young breast. The study in Hiroshima, Japan, of the women who developed breast cancer 20 years after the atomic bomb was dropped on the city at the end of the Second World War is frequently quoted, but it is not only Hiroshima that points up the role of ionizing radiation. There is a mass of evidence, recently published by the American scientist John Gofman, to suggest that medical radiation for various conditions in the past half-century, including the mass screening programme for tuberculosis, may be responsible for the current epidemic of breast cancer. While not denying that breast cancer is usually multifactorial in origin, he comes to the devastating conclusion that up to 75 per cent of recent breast cancers in America would not have happened without an earlier history of breast irradiation – medical and other.

What also has not received sufficient attention is the risk from radiation fall-out. The above-ground nuclear tests in the 1950s and accidents like Chernobyl in the 1980s may be exacting their price now.

● **Diethylstilboestrol (DES)**, a synthetic oestrogen, given to women in the 1940s, 1950s and 1960s to prevent miscarriage and stop their milk after childbirth if they did not want to breastfeed. Both these groups of women are

Who gets breast cancer?

Under the age of 30 you are unlikely to develop breast cancer, but there are still nearly 500 cases a year in this age group, so be vigilant.

known to be at significantly higher risk of developing breast cancer in later life.

The hormonal link, specifically the endogenous (naturally occurring) hormones oestrogen and progesterone we produce in our bodies every month, is very important. Prolonged exposure of the breast to oestrogen appears to increase the risk of breast cancer. Thus a woman who started her periods early, has no children, or has them only towards the end of her reproductive life, and then concludes with a late menopause, is more at risk than a woman with a reverse menstrual pattern.

Exogenous (external supplementary) hormones, like DES and those used in the contraceptive pill and in hormone replacement therapy (HRT), also increase risk. A woman who takes the contraceptive pill when young and before becoming pregnant increases her risk of breast cancer prior to the menopause. Whether the risk continues after the menopause has not yet been established. Taking HRT to supplement the failing ovaries at menopause, over a ten-to-fifteen-year period, also increases the risk, but not by as much as having a late menopause.

Heredity

The inherited genetic connection accounts for somewhere between 5 and 10 per cent of breast cancer cases annually. It has been known for a long time that women with a family history of breast cancer, particularly in first-degree relatives – a mother, sister or daughter – are at increased risk. And the younger the relative or relatives at the time of diagnosis, the greater the risk becomes. For example, a woman whose sister developed breast cancer before the age of 40 has a cumulative 10 per cent increased risk of developing the disease herself before she is 65. The risk increases to 25 per cent if she has two relatives with breast cancer, at least one of whom was diagnosed before she was 50.

So far only two hereditary breast cancer genes have been identified: BRCA1 and BRCA2. It will soon be possible to offer a diagnostic blood test for BRCA1 which is responsible for about one-third of familial breast cancers, and possibly some other cancers too. This gene can be transmitted through either parent and some family members may be carriers and pass it on without developing the disease themselves.

Cancer of many types is now thought to be a genetic disease. Research on another important gene, P53, responsible for controlling cell growth throughout the body, has revealed that it is sometimes damaged or missing in many people who develop common cancers, including breast cancer. There may be several other similar 'predisposing' genes which, if they sustain a lesion (damage or loss of function) for whatever reason, cause cell damage and ultimately a cancer.

The hope from research now in progress is that in addition to answering our many questions about the inheritance factor and how the potential ill effects can be countermanded, we will also discover why it is that some 'good' genes turn into cancer oncogenes. Something switches them on to make them mutate and become defective, causing breast cancer in women without a family history. These different gene behaviours indicate how complex the problem is.

Who gets breast cancer?

Family cancer tree

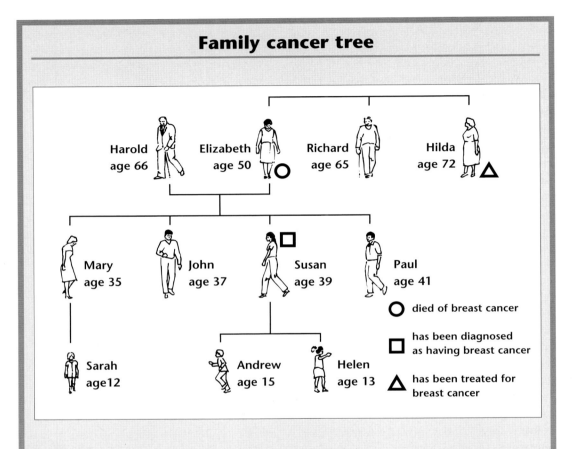

Harold age 66 — Elizabeth age 50 ○ — Richard age 65 — Hilda age 72 △

Mary age 35 — John age 37 — Susan age 39 □ — Paul age 41

Sarah age 12 — Andrew age 15 — Helen age 13

○ died of breast cancer

□ has been diagnosed as having breast cancer

△ has been treated for breast cancer

Inherited risk

This family shows evidence of carrying a breast cancer gene that can be inherited from either parent. Elizabeth died from breast cancer when she was 50 years old. Hilda is alive at age 72, having been treated for breast cancer when she was 64. Susan developed the disease when she was aged 39.

Screening

Mary has a 1 in 2 lifetime risk of inheriting the susceptibility to breast cancer and her chance of developing the disease is 1 in 3. She would be offered a mammogram and then yearly screening by ultrasound until she was 40. Then she would have a yearly mammogram and at age 50 she could join the national screening programme.

Family cancer tree

We do not know if Mary will develop breast cancer, so her daughter (Sarah) has a 1 in 4 chance of inheriting the susceptibility to the disease. Helen's risk, however, is 1 in 2 because her mother is affected. Both Sarah and Helen would not be offered screening until they were 25. Then they could take part in a programme like Mary's.

Cancer test

Researchers are looking to find the faulty gene and then hope to develop a test. Those who have inherited the gene could be identified, followed up and offered screening. Those who have not could be reassured.

Who should have the genetic test?

It is all very well to ask for the genetic test, when it becomes available, but what will you do with the resulting knowledge? A woman told she does not carry the gene will obviously feel relief for herself and her daughters. But this does not guarantee that she will never develop breast cancer from some other cause. The woman told that she does have the BRCA1 gene will be burdened with fear for herself and her daughters for the rest of her life. She now knows for certain that she is genetically programmed for breast cancer, but no one can predict with any certainty whether or not she will ultimately develop the disease. She can only be given risk estimates.

Almost worse for many women would be the fear this knowledge gives them that they may already have passed on the disease to one or more of their daughters. Good counselling is essential to support a woman while she absorbs the implications of this unwelcome knowledge. She will also need skilled support to be available to her while she considers her personal options for preventive measures, including possibly treatment.

There are now cancer family clinics for people at high genetic risk. If you think you fall into this risk category, ask your family doctor to refer you.

At such a clinic you will be kept under careful surveillance. A full family history going back at least three generations will be taken. The Imperial Cancer Research Fund recommends that the high-risk woman be given a physical examination every year and offered five-yearly mammograms from the age of 30, reducing to every two years from age 37 and yearly from the age of 50. Obviously you should report immediately any abnormal change occurring during the interval between your yearly visits to the clinic.

Who gets breast cancer?

Guidelines for referral to a family history clinic for breast cancer

● Mother or sister developed breast cancer when aged less than 40.

● Mother or sister developed breast cancer before the age of 50, and another close relative on the same side of the family developed cancer of the breast, ovary, colon or endometrium (womb lining), or a sarcoma, before the age of 65.

● Mother or sister developed breast cancer when aged 50–65, and one other close relative on the same side of the family developed one of the above cancers.

● Mother or sister developed double primary cancer (of the breast and another cancer as above); at least one of the tumours occurred before the age of 50 and the breast cancer occurred before the age of 65.

● Dominant history of breast cancer (four or more cases of breast and/or ovarian cancer, on the same side of the family at any age).

● History of related malignancy in mother or father (cancer of colorectum, ovary or endometrium, or a sarcoma, before the age of 50), and at least one of their first-degree relatives developed breast cancer before the age of 50.

● Two or more cases of related types (as above) in close relatives on father's side, but not necessarily including father, with one cancer diagnosed before the age of 50.

(*Source: British Medical Journal* 1994, 308, 183–7.)

It is known that heredity plays a part in 5 to 10 per cent of women unfortunate enough to develop breast cancer.

Other risk factors

Other possible risk factors include:

- environmental hazards (such as pesticides);
- lifestyle (diet and alcohol intake);
- obesity;
- stress.

Studies in America and Israel have linked the use of certain pesticides with a rise in breast cancer. Other studies indicate that areas with chemical waste sites show a marked increase in incidence. There are fears too about the effects of electro-magnetic fields. We already have abundant evidence indicating that chemical pollutants enter the food chain, infiltrate our water and settle in human fatty tissue, but we can still only speculate as to their effect on the breast cancer rates. What we urgently now need from our scientists is a wide-ranging long-term investigation into the effect this ubiquitous contamination could be having on everyone's genetic make-up and possibly on the health of future generations.

A high-fat diet is commonly cited as a risk factor, but the evidence is conflicting. Is it the type of fat which counts – saturated animal fat as opposed to monounsaturated fats found in olive oil, avocadoes and oily fish – or is it what fat does to oestrogen? Meat eaters apparently reabsorb oestrogen more efficiently than vegetarians and consequently have much higher levels of circulating oestrogen in their blood. Obesity, particularly after the menopause, puts women at risk because body fat itself produces oestrogen. Another theory suggests that fat tissue and the toxins embedded in it may interact dangerously.

There are about 30 studies examining the

A low-fat diet is believed by some to reduce the risk of developing breast cancer, though the evidence is conflicting.

link between alcohol and breast cancer and there appears to be an increased risk when consumption exceeds the recommended amount of 14 units per week. Even two units taken at certain times in the menstrual cycle can apparently raise oestrogen levels by 30 per cent. Epidemiologists are divided among themselves as to whether it is the alcohol alone or interaction with some other dietary element that produces this effect.

Stress is another speculative area. Studies

Who gets breast cancer?

suggest that women at either end of the emotional spectrum who either always firmly put the lid on their feelings, particularly anger, or, alternatively, frequently lose their temper, are more at risk. Then there are the many recorded cases of women who discover a lump which is subsequently diagnosed as breast cancer soon after some severe personal trauma in their lives like bereavement or a divorce. Stress may not directly cause the disease, but it might be the trigger which causes a 'good' gene to go rogue and become an oncogene. Given the effect stress is known to produce on

hormonal function and our immune system, would this be so surprising?

How are we to judge risk for ourselves? We can easily frighten ourselves silly by ticking off the checklists below and finding we fit the high-risk profile. Yet we may never get breast cancer. And there are many apparently low-risk women who are shocked and distressed to discover they have it.

Remember that 70 per cent of women diagnosed with breast cancer will not conform to the high-risk profile. That proportion fits with the widely accepted estimate that

Studies have shown a link between alcohol and breast cancer when alcohol consumption exceeds the recommended 14 units per week.

approximately 70 per cent of all cancers may have an environmental cause; 35 per cent of these may be connected with diet. Is there any reason to think that breast cancer, a complex but nonetheless common cancer, should be markedly different in its aetiology (causation)? We need more research in these areas.

Risk indicators for breast cancer

Low-risk woman:
- Has no family history of breast cancer.
- Has a late menarche (onset of periods).
- Has long menstrual cycles, i.e. more than 30 days.
- Has one or more babies in her late teens/early twenties.
- Completes her family before 35.
- Breastfeeds for at least three months.
- Doesn't take the pill before her first pregnancy.
- Has an early natural menopause (mid-forties) or bilateral oopherectomy (removal of both ovaries) before 35.
- Does not take HRT.
- Eats a vegetarian low-fat diet.
- Drinks moderately or not at all.
- Is slim and active.
- Has an equable temperament.
- Is not exposed to stressful life events.

High-risk woman:
- Had a previous cancer in her other breast.
- Has a history of benign breast disease showing cell change.
- Has a blood relative (mother, sister or daughter) with breast cancer before menopause.
- Has a family history of breast and ovarian cancer (either parent).
- Has an early menarche (before 11).
- Takes the pill for at least four years when young and before her first pregnancy.
- Has her first or last child late (after 35).
- Has no children.
- Has a late menopause (after 54).
- Takes HRT.
- Eats a diet high in saturated fat.
- Drinks more than two units of alcohol a day.
- Is overweight.

Chapter three

Prevention
and screening

To date there is no effective preventive treatment for breast cancer other than the drastic measure of prophylactic bilateral mastectomy. This means removing every scrap of breast tissue from both breasts, usually with immediate breast reconstruction. A small but growing number of British women who are at exceptionally high risk for family reasons have been prepared, after careful counselling, to go so far. Even this may not always work.

Something is better than nothing

Prevention of breast cancer will not be possible until we have a better understanding of what causes it, but this does not mean that we cannot take some sensible precautions. Draw up your own risk profile and see whether there is anything you can modify.

Genes

You have no control over your genetic inheritance, but if you know that your family history puts you at high risk, ask your doctor to refer you to a cancer family clinic where you will be carefully monitored and counselled.

Lifestyle/diet

The evidence is unequivocal. A low-fat high-fibre diet including plenty of fruit and vegetables is good for your all-round health. Heart, bones, other organs, your immune system and your mental state will all benefit from this diet and it may prevent cancer.

Several studies now in progress are measuring the benefits of vitamin and mineral supplements. A recently published five-year study of 30,000 Chinese has shown that a combination of beta-carotenes, vitamin E and the mineral selenium significantly reduces the cancer risk. Vitamin C is also thought to be important.

Beta-carotenes are crucial. In addition to being necessary for producing vitamin A, they appear to have an antioxidant role. Basically they inactivate a chemical molecule called singlet oxygen which, if left unchecked in the body, generates free radicals (these can cause cell damage). Their second line of attack, probably in conjunction with vitamin E (another important antioxidant), is to trap and destroy free radicals circulating in the system which are encouraged by smoking, air pollution, heavy drinking, pesticides, UVA rays from the sun and even strenuous exercise.

Dietary recommendations

● Eat daily at least 400g/1lb of fruit and vegetables – a minimum of five portions – ideally organically or home-grown.

● Include daily 15–25mg of beta-carotene; this is present in carrots, spinach, spring greens, watercress, tomatoes, broccoli, parsley, sweet potatoes, cantaloupe melon, apricots and peaches.

● Include recommended amounts of all vitamins, but especially vitamins C and E. Vitamin C is found in citrus fruits, potatoes, cabbage, kale, spinach, tomatoes and watercress. Vitamin E is present in nuts and seeds, wholegrain cereals, wheatgerm and vegetable oils like sunflower and corn oil.

● Include a trace element of selenium, which is found in seafood, liver and in grains and seeds grown in soil.

● Cut down on saturated animal fats containing selenium found in meat, dairy products, cakes and biscuits.

● Keep your alcohol intake within the recommended 14 units per week for women (see page 26).

To help guard against breast cancer, eat at least five portions of fresh fruit and vegetables every day.

Prevention and screening

A good varied diet should not need supplementation but we do not know how much of our food loses its nutritional value on the long journey from growing to selling. If you have any doubts or know you could be at risk of vitamin deficiency because you are a smoker, elderly or on a diet, take a multi-vitamin supplement. You cannot overdose on beta-carotenes – your body converts to vitamin A only what it needs. Most beta-carotene supplements are synthetic; look on the label for the ingredient dunaliella or 'd' salina if you want a natural one.

Natural hormones

There is not much you can do about your menstrual pattern, except perhaps try to alter the frequency of your periods. A British study has shown that adding 60mg of soya protein to the daily diet can increase the length of a woman's menstrual cycle by two to six days. A longer cycle (a Japanese woman's 32 days, say, instead of the British woman's average 27 days) reduces hormonal stimulation of the breast, a suspected cause. Soya also produces a weak oestrogen which, research suggests, may suppress the growth-producing effects of oestradiol (the body's natural oestrogen).

Synthetic hormones

Think again about the hormones you take. The condom is the safest contraceptive we have in these Aids-aware times, so perhaps it would be all-round good advice for our daughters to suggest that they insist on the condom and use the pill with caution until after they have had their first child. Career patterns too may need

It might be healthier for women to have children early in their working life rather than waiting to establish themselves in their chosen career before childbearing.

reconsidering. Should we not be making it easier for women to have children early in their working life rather than, as now, waiting to establish themselves before taking a break for childbearing, by which time their biological clock has almost run down?

Meanwhile there are studies under way to see whether a preventative agent could be added to the contraceptive pill. Melatonin, a hormone that controls seasonal reproduction in animals, and gestodene, a synthetic progestogen, already used in some contraceptive pills, both appear to prevent breast cells proliferating after ovulation, but we will have to wait at least ten years for a definitive answer.

A study in California has overtones of *Stepford Wives* manipulation. A small group of women in their twenties and thirties at high family risk for breast cancer are taking a monthly dose of a contraceptive hormone called gonadotropin-releasing hormone agonist (GNRHA) which inhibits ovulation by shutting down the ovaries. Neither oestrogen nor progesterone is produced. Unfortunately, it causes menopausal side effects, including bone loss and infertility, which then have to be reversed by a feedback of testosterone, carefully regulated oestrogen replacement therapy for 24 days out of 28, and progesterone for 13 days every fourth month to induce a period.

Must you take HRT?

HRT protects against heart disease and osteoporosis in later life, which is why many doctors recommend it to women. It also provides relief for many women from unpleasant menopausal symptoms like hot flushes, night sweats, mood swings and vaginal dryness, but it does not suit everyone. Current research indicates that taking it for ten years or longer causes a 'modest' increased risk of breast cancer, regardless of your risk status.

Say you are already at a slightly increased risk because you started your periods early, took the pill in your teens and had a child after the age of 35: it might be sensible to pause when you are offered HRT at the menopause, especially if you have no troublesome symptoms. Even if you do have symptoms, there are homeopathic remedies and mineral and vitamin supplements available from health-food shops which you could try first. It seems a dubious logic to be taking a hormone supplement to reduce the risk of one disease only to increase the risk for another, equally life-threatening one.

The problem for women trying to make up their minds about HRT is that they are faced with a mass of conflicting evidence which tends to raise more questions than it answers. One fact is clear, however: women who retain their uterus should take the combined version, containing progestogen as well as oestrogen, to protect them against the risk of endometrial cancer. The endometrium (lining of the womb) thickens and may become cancerous with oestrogen-only therapy. Yet the combined pill may be a higher risk for breast cancer. Another study suggests that how it is given may be important. Taking it by injection, instead of as an implant or by tablet, seems to raise the risk, though no one can say why. And, final irony, women who develop breast cancer while on HRT have a better prognosis, according to one American study.

Prevention and screening

To have or not to have HRT? For middle-aged women the evidence is still contradictory.

The Tamoxifen prevention trial

This trial is a five-year study involving 16,000 women in the USA and 14,000 women in Britain. A similar multicentre trial has also started in Italy, but involving only women who have had a hysterectomy (see pages 50–1 for information on side effects). Although there are variable entry criteria in different countries, the basic premise of the overall trial is that Tamoxifen, an anti-oestrogen which has been used for some years to treat women with breast cancer (see Chapter five), might also work as a preventative agent. An overview of 40 trials has shown that it reduces mortality by 11 per cent

in early breast cancer. It also offers a 40 per cent chance of preventing a subsequent cancer in the other breast, and is believed to delay recurrence in many cases. A pilot Tamoxifen prevention study begun in 1986 at the Royal Marsden Hospital in London has so far enrolled 2,000 women under less strict entry criteria; interim results only have been reported so far. About 25 per cent of women have dropped out.

The women eligible for this innovative multicentre trial must be at high risk for breast cancer and understand that they will be randomized either to Tamoxifen or a placebo for five years. It is double blind which means that neither doctor nor woman knows which tablet she is receiving. Women entering the trial will be given regular health checks every six months.

Entry criteria for the UK trial
For women aged 35–39:
● two or more close relatives (mother, sisters or daughters) who developed breast cancer at age 50 or less;
● mother, sister or daughter who developed cancer in both breasts with first cancer diagnosed at 40 or less;

For women aged 40–44, the same as above plus:
● having no children *and* a mother or sister who developed breast cancer at age 40 or less;
● having had a benign biopsy with signs of proliferative cell change *and* a mother, sister or daughter who developed breast cancer at age 40 or less;
● atypical ductal or lobular hyperplasia (changes in cell structure) diagnosed at biopsy.

For women aged 45–65, the same as above, but there is no age limit on when close relatives, including an aunt or a grandmother, developed breast cancer.

Contraindications for entry

For women who:
- are pregnant or want to become pregnant;
- have had a previous cancer;
- have been or are on Tamoxifen;
- are on long-term HRT;
- have had a pulmonary embolism or deep-vein thrombosis;
- have some other medical condition more serious than the risk of breast cancer or have a life expectancy of less than ten years.

This is a controversial trial because it requires healthy women to commit themselves to the possibility of taking a drug for experimental purposes for five years. There is no such thing as a drug without side effects. Most of the Tamoxifen side effects are relatively minor, especially when compared with the side effects of chemotherapy for the treatment of breast cancer, or indeed the long-term outcome for inadequately treated breast cancer. However, menopausal symptoms like hot flushes, weight gain and vaginal discharge may not seem so minor to a woman who was previously enjoying good health. Other side effects are more serious: there is a two-to-three-fold increased risk of endometrial cancer which can usually be treated by hysterectomy, but deaths have occurred. Visual disorders, serious complications in the blood circulation and liver damage, including two cases of liver cancer,

have also been reported.

If you are high risk for breast cancer and think you might like to enter this trial, it is sensible to inform yourself as thoroughly as possible about Tamoxifen. Ask your doctor for the detailed information document which summarizes all the Tamoxifen studies, reporting results, side effects and some additional benefits. For example, it seems that Tamoxifen may reduce heart disease and bone loss in postmenopausal women.

Screening

Screening for breast cancer cannot prevent the disease occurring, but it can detect very early cancers, tumours often so small that neither a woman nor her doctor can feel them. This early detection means that the cancer can be treated at a stage when cure is much more likely.

The NHS breast-screening programme began in 1990 and currently screens more than 1.6 million women aged between 50 and 64 every year – one-third of the target group. The lower age limit is based on data from several screening trials around the world which indicates that mammography (X-ray of the breast) is more effective for postmenopausal women.

In 1992 the government set the following target for breast cancer in its White Paper, *The Health of the Nation*: 'To reduce the death rate for breast cancer in the population invited for screening by at least 25 per cent by the year 2000 (from 95.1 per 100,000 population in 1990 to no more than 71.3 per 100,000).'

This could mean 1,250 lives saved each year – but only if enough women continue to

Prevention and screening

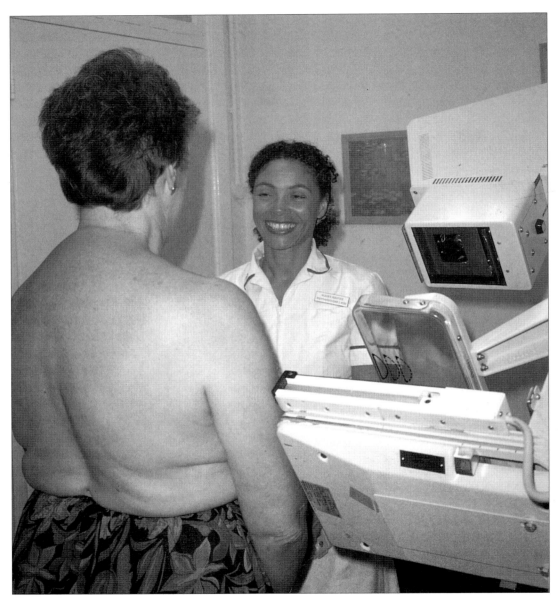

Screening by mammography can detect breast cancer at a very early stage, making a cure much more likely.

respond to the invitation. Country women appear to be keener than women living in urban areas. Part of the reason for the wide discrepancies in uptake (it must be 70 per cent or higher to keep the programme cost-effective) may be because inner-city women tend to move more often and family doctors' records may not be as good.

  Why aren't women under the age of 50 screened?

 The breast tissue of younger women before the menopause is much more dense and difficult to X-ray. However, there is a major randomized trial in progress at the moment involving some 65,000 women all over the country aged between 40 and 49 to see whether screening every year picks up a significant extra number of cancers. Their progress is being compared with a control group of 130,000 women who are not being offered screening until 50. We will not have a complete answer to this question until after the year 2000.

 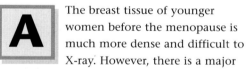 **Why aren't women over the age of 64 being screened?**

The official answer is that older women are reluctant to present themselves. Unofficially it means spending more money. However,

all women over the age of 64, with their increased risk of developing breast cancer, can and should ask to be included in the screening programme. Most recent figures for those in this older age group who do refer themselves for screening show that the rate of cancer detection is more than double that for younger screened women. Fourteen cancers per 1,000 women were detected in the 65-plus age group compared with six cancers per 1,000 in women aged between 50 and 64.

 How can I get on to the screening programme?

Make sure that your family doctor has your correct address and, if you move, be certain to register with a new doctor. Provided your doctor has your correct address you will be automatically invited to come for screening as soon as you reach the age of 50.

 How often will I be screened?

 At the moment it is every three years, but research is currently in progress at five centres to see whether the intervals should be reduced to two years, or even less. It is very important to respond to all the invitations you receive. Screening could save your life.

Prevention and screening

Is there any risk from radiation?

Minimal. The estimated risk of a radiation-induced cancer with the current dose is one per million women over 50 after a ten-year latent period. By contrast, in an unscreened population there would be 1,400 spontaneous cancers per year per million women at age 50 and 2,000 per year per million women at age 65. Mammograms should, however, be used as sparingly as is consistent with good practice.

What happens at a screening clinic?

You will be given an appointment time in your letter of invitation which you can always change if it is inconvenient. Screening units are either hospital-based or in a mobile unit parked accessibly in a supermarket forecourt or town centre. Many health authorities organize free transport to bring women in from rural areas.

There are usually two radiographers running a mobile unit who divide the work of taking a medical history and doing the mammograms. Appointments are made for every ten minutes, so there may be other women waiting in the reception area. This should not stop you asking any questions you want to ask.

Once your address and other personal details have been taken you will be shown into a curtained dressing room and asked to strip to the waist, so choose that morning to wear a blouse and skirt, or trousers, rather than a frock. Now into the mammography area where the radiographer places each breast in turn on a plastic shelf and then compresses it with a metal or plastic 'plate' as tightly as you can bear, to take the picture. The whole procedure lasts only a few minutes, but some women do find it quite uncomfortable. After dressing you will be told to expect your results shortly – most centres send them within a week, and it certainly will not be more than a fortnight.

Before you go you will be given some breast awareness literature and reminded that you must always report any changes immediately. More than three out of four women will be very relieved a few days later by their letter telling them that they are in the clear, though of course this does not mean that they can relax the good habit of checking their breasts regularly.

Some women will be asked to come back for further tests. This naturally causes the individual woman a great deal of anxiety, yet in the majority of cases it will prove to be a false alarm. It may turn out to have been a technical problem with the mammogram, or there may be some uncertainty about the 'abnormality' on the mammogram which proves to have a benign cause.

Chapter four

Assessment and diagnosis

Please come back

Approximately 5 per cent of the women who are screened each year will be asked to return for further tests. The letter asking them to attend their local Assessment Clinic will undoubtedly make them very anxious. However, should it happen to you, do keep the appointment. As the figures in the table on the right show, in most cases it will turn out to be a false alarm. Even if you are one of the unlucky few to be diagnosed with a cancer, your chances of making a good recovery are so much better for having it detected at an early stage. You can also be sure that you will receive a high standard of treatment.

Screening activity for 1992/93

(All women aged 50 and over)	
Women invited	1,612,450
Women screened	1,165,726
(includes self-and GP referrals)	
Women recalled	63,076
Breast biopsies	9,129
Cancers detected	6,597
Cancers 1cm/^{3}/4in or less	1,497

What happens at an Assessment Clinic?

If the problem is a simple technical one – for instance, the first mammogram taken in the screening clinic may have produced an unsatisfactory picture – a new mammogram will be done and read immediately by the radiologist. You may also be given a clinical (physical) examination. If all is well, you will be back in the normal screening programme.

Early (first-stage) diagnosis

If, however, the doubt raised was clinical because the mammogram appears to show an abnormality, you will be given a full range of tests: a clinical examination, another mammogram and probably an ultrasound too, which is particularly good for distinguishing cysts from other lesions. At this stage the

Assessment and diagnosis

medical team examining you – the surgeon, radiologist and cytopathologist – will probably decide that you should also have a fine needle aspiration (FNA).

The skilled freehand version of FNA can be done as described on page 16 when the doctor can feel a lump. However, some lesions picked up on a mammogram can neither be felt nor easily located. In such cases FNA is done by

using either ultrasound or the new stereotactic technique which guides a hollow core needle into the centre of the lesion by computer imaging. This latter procedure is quite taxing because you have to sit absolutely still for between 20 and 30 minutes.

The liquid and cellular matter drawn off by FNA can be analysed within 30 minutes and a result given to you. If it is benign, you will be

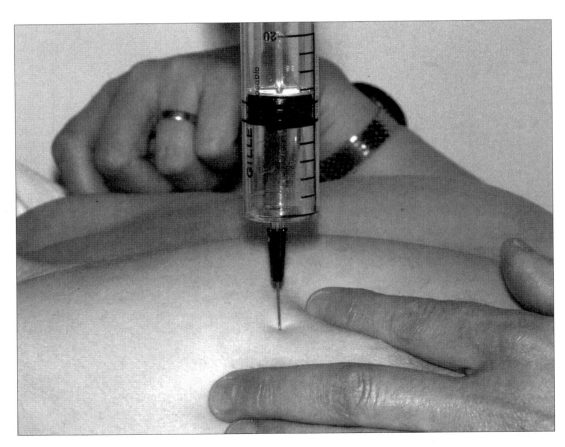

A doctor performing a fine needle aspiration.

able to leave the clinic feeling reassured. Even so, you may be asked to return for another screen in six months' time if the doctors feel that there may be signs of an early cell change in the breast. This process where the cells begin to multiply (proliferate) is called hyperplasia. It may not develop into anything serious but the Assessment Clinic will want to keep you under supervision.

FNA is a type of biopsy which has become very popular because it causes so little trauma and gives an immediate result. Currently research is in progress in the UK at Nottingham City Hospital to see whether FNA samples can be minutely analysed, using new technology to test for recognized prognostic factors which predict the future behaviour of the cancer.

In some cancers the FNA will be followed by a surgical biopsy to remove more tissue for further analysis. This can be done under local or general anaesthetic and the tissue sample will be sent to the pathologist. You will have to wait a few days for a result – obviously an anxious period. Women who are seen in an Assessment Clinic are usually able to talk to a breast care nurse who has been trained as a counsellor and can answer their questions.

For women who are not in the breast screening programme (and who are prepared to be assertive)

What should I do if I discover a suspicious change in my breast?

Mammograms, ultrasound, clinical examination and biopsies are all available in specialist breast clinics for symptomatic women. Report your problem immediately to your family doctor and ask to be referred as soon as possible to such a centre. Your doctor should have a directory of NHS breast care services which has been supplied to every general practice in the UK, free of charge, by the Cancer Relief Macmillan Fund.

What if my family doctor says that he or she does not have a contract with a local hospital offering such a service, or that he or she prefers to refer me to a surgeon of his or her choice at another hospital with no specialized breast service?

Say that you want to go to a clinic where you know that everyone has specialist experience of breast cancer.

If this does not convince your doctor, show him or her the ten minimum standards of care for breast cancer laid down by the Cancer Relief Macmillan Fund (see page 7). Remind your doctor that the first standard states: 'Every woman should have a prompt referral by a family doctor to a team specializing in the diagnosis and treatment of breast cancer, including a consultant from within the team.'

You can ask to see the specialist leading the team at your first consultation, or later for any reason, but especially if you are unhappy about the advice you are receiving.

Assessment and diagnosis

Key features of a specialist breast unit

● Handles 50 minimum but preferably many more cases of breast cancer annually.
● Medical core team includes consultant surgeon, consultant radiologist, consultant histopathologist/cytologist, consultant oncologist, chemotherapy specialist nurse, a breast care nurse specialist and a diagnostic radiographer.
● Has adequate facilities on site and access to all other necessary services, including additional medical staff – psychologists, physiotherapists, pharmacists, etc.
● Adheres to locally agreed guidelines for care and regularly audits outcomes.
● Participates in trials and other research.
(*Source*: Condensed from a report on provision of breast services by the British Breast Group, 1994.)

 Q What if I am told that my hospital appointment will be in several weeks' time?

 A Remind your doctor that the second standard states: 'Every woman should have a firm diagnosis within four weeks of being referred to a hospital by a family doctor.' So ask your doctor to ring the hospital and insist that you be seen at the next clinic.

 Q What if the hospital doctor tells me that I will have to wait several weeks for a diagnosis?

 A Do not accept this and repeat the second standard to him or her as above.

 Q What if the surgeon says that he or she prefers to do a surgical biopsy, send the frozen section of tissue down to the laboratory for analysis, and then proceed immediately with a mastectomy if it proves to be cancerous?

 A You do not have to accept this if you do not want to. Remind your doctor that the third standard states: 'Every woman should have the opportunity of a confirmed diagnosis before consenting to treatment, including surgery.'

Confirmed (second-stage) diagnosis

A detailed confirmed (that is, definite) diagnosis should include detailed analysis of the tumour. This is important because it gives doctors some essential pointers for prognosis; the knowledge helps them to decide on the most appropriate treatment plan.

Types of cancer

Below are brief descriptions of types of cancer.
● **In situ** (usually ductal, but 10 per cent are

lobular) means that cancer cells have grown but have not penetrated the breast membrane. These very early cancers are now found much more often as a result of screening with mammography. If left untreated, some, though not all, of these *in situ* cancers will become invasive.

● **Invasive** means the tumour is spreading to surrounding tissue. There are many different types of invasive breast cancer arising in different parts of the breast. The most common is infiltrating ductal carcinoma (about 75 per cent of all breast cancers). Some of the less common types of invasive cancer have a better long-term prognosis.

● **Inflammatory** cancer usually makes itself apparent with a rash and the breast feels hot, swollen and painful. This tends to be a cancer of rapid growth, often called aggressive.

Deciding what stage a cancer has reached

Staging is determined by size of tumour and extent of spread. The stages are as follows:

● **Stage 0** *In situ.*

● **Stage I** Tumour less than 2cm/¾in. No spread.

● **Stage IIA** Tumour 2cm/¾in or smaller and has spread to axillary (armpit) lymph nodes (glands); or tumour 2–5cm/¾–2in but no spread.

● **Stage IIB** Tumour 2–5cm/¾–2in and has spread to axillary lymph nodes; tumour more than 5cm/2in but has not spread to lymph nodes or more distant parts of body.

● **Stage IIIA** Tumour 2–5cm/¾–2in and has spread to several axillary lymph nodes, causing them to stick together; or more than 5cm/2in and has spread to axillary lymph nodes.

● **Stage IIIB** Tumour any size but is fixed either to chest wall or muscle, or involves lymphatics of skin or skin itself, and may or may not involve axillary lymph nodes; or tumour any size but has spread to lymph nodes above collar bone.

● **Stage IV** Tumour any size; lymph nodes may or may not be involved, but cancer has spread to areas other than breast and lymph nodes. (*Source of definitions*: International Union against Cancer.)

Other prognostic features

There are several other prognostic tests that can be done, including most usually oestrogen and progesterone receptor status; and DNA (primary genetic material). A positive oestrogen or progesterone receptor result means that the tumour is sensitive to hormone treatment. The DNA analysis indicates what is happening with the breast cancer cells and how rapidly they are growing or dividing.

Bad news

Some women are going to hear the words we all dread: 'I'm sorry to tell you that you have a cancer'. Not all doctors are good communicators; even the most well-meaning can get it wrong sometimes and there are some who, to put it mildly, are not gifted with words.

Assessment and diagnosis

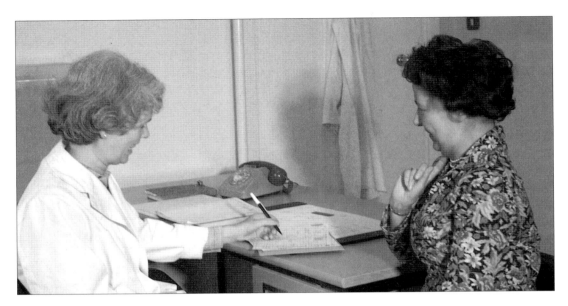

Not all doctors are good communicators, but training in communication skills is now becoming available to them.

At least there is now widespread recognition within the medical profession that a problem exists. At every level, from senior doctors to medical students, training in communication skills is now becoming available, generally on an optional basis, so it will take time for the benefits to percolate. Meanwhile there are thousands of individual women who are still being told the bad news carelessly, casually or callously.

It is difficult to protect yourself against something you are not expecting. Probably the best thing you can do for yourself, or offer as advice to someone else, is always to ask a person who is close to you to accompany you on a visit to a specialist clinic. That way you can be sure of support from someone who cares for you, should you need it. Their presence may also serve to make the doctor more conscious of the words that he or she uses.

The woman diagnosed with breast cancer faces an unknown journey into a new and frightening country. You will be engulfed by emotions fighting to take the upper hand; by turns you will be feeling fearful, angry, depressed, despairing and helpless.

Information is a powerful tool to help you regain some measure of control over your life. If you have read this far, you probably want to find out all you can about how to fight your disease. On your journey keep the Macmillan minimum standards to hand (see page 7) so that you can check you are receiving all you have a right to expect.

Chapter five

Treatments for early breast cancer

Some breast clinics now aim to be 'one-stop diagnostic' which means that any woman presenting with symptoms can be given a diagnosis, good or bad, before the end of the day. This is wonderful for the woman who leaves the clinic with a clean bill of health, feeling immeasurably relieved because she has been told her symptoms are benign. It is not quite as simple for the woman with a diagnosis of cancer. As we saw in Chapter four, her biopsy sample will probably need further careful analysis before the medical team can really begin to consider her treatment options.

Precisely because breast cancer is so complex and variable, even the most experienced doctors are still far from achieving consensus on what is the 'best' treatment for every case presented to them. To the individual woman this can be both bewildering and disturbing. Aren't doctors the experts? Don't they always know what the treatment should be? Why are there so many different treatments?

The answer frankly, where it concerns breast cancer, is ambivalent. Yes, the specialists know a lot, much more than those who see only a few breast cancer patients a year, but the more they know, the less they know they know. This honest uncertainty underscores the value for the patient of being treated by a team of skilled professionals who can pool their expertise at regular meetings where they are not afraid to discuss their problems openly.

Don't be afraid to ask for information – or to say 'no'

That said, in many cases the treatment options will be relatively straightforward and the doctors can make their recommendations without too much heartsearching. It is, however, important that each individual woman should feel free to ask for as much information as she wants.

Remember the fifth and sixth Macmillan standards: 'Every woman should have: full

information about types of surgery (including breast reconstruction where appropriate) and the role of medical treatments (for example, radiotherapy, chemotherapy, Tamoxifen); and a full explanation about the aims of the treatments proposed and their benefits and possible side effects.' You do not have to accept the advice offered you, or you may want a second opinion. It is your body; your decision.

Treatments for early breast cancer

We are all different. Some women want to know everything they can about their disease and expect to be fully involved in making decisions about their treatment. Others may want to be well informed about what is going on, but are happy to leave the treatment choices to their doctors. And there is a third group who really want to get through the whole business knowing as little as possible and leaving all the decisions to their doctors.

Whatever your personal bias, every woman should be aware that she does not have to be rushed into treatment. The bad old days when women were whisked into hospital overnight and into the operating theatre not knowing whether they would wake up with a breast removed have gone. A few extra days to think about what you really want and a chance to discuss your options with your partner or family will make no difference to the progress of the disease. Remember the seventh Macmillan standard: 'Every woman should have as much time as she needs to consider treatment options.'

Standard treatments for early breast cancer

Your doctors have two aims when treating you for an early breast cancer (stages 0–IIB):
1 to eradicate the local disease – that is, get rid of the cancerous area in the breast and remove any infected lymph nodes;
2 to destroy by systemic or adjuvant (supplementary) therapy any cancerous cells that may have already escaped undetected (micrometastases) into your body through the bloodstream or the lymphatics.

First (primary) treatment

Primary treatment is usually surgery followed by postoperative radiotherapy to mop up any cancer cells that may have been left behind.

Surgery

There are two main types of operation:
- **a total mastectomy**, in which all breast tissue is removed, is usually either a **simple mastectomy**, which removes the breast tissue alone and is sometimes immediately followed by breast reconstruction using an implant (see page 60), or a **modified radical mastectomy**, which removes all breast tissue together with some or all of the underlying chest muscle and lymph nodes;
- **a partial mastectomy** ranging from **lumpectomy** (local excision), in which the lump only is removed together with a small amount of surrounding tissue, to

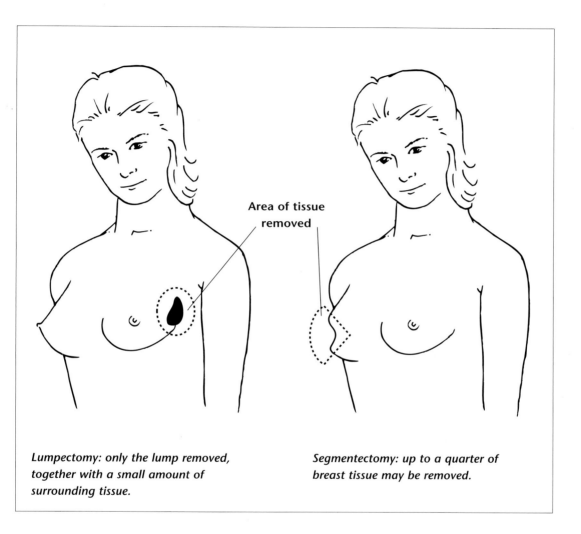

Area of tissue removed

Lumpectomy: only the lump removed, together with a small amount of surrounding tissue.

Segmentectomy: up to a quarter of breast tissue may be removed.

segmentectomy (wide local excision) to **quadrantectomy**, in which at least a quarter of the breast is removed.

The type of partial mastectomy a doctor chooses to do should be based on an assessment of the sort of cancer you have, the size of the lump and how much surrounding tissue needs to be removed with the lump. The doctor aims to conserve as much of the breast as possible without increasing your risk of recurrence.

Studies have shown that long-term survival rates are the same in early breast cancer whether you have mastectomy or lumpectomy.

45

Treatments for early breast cancer

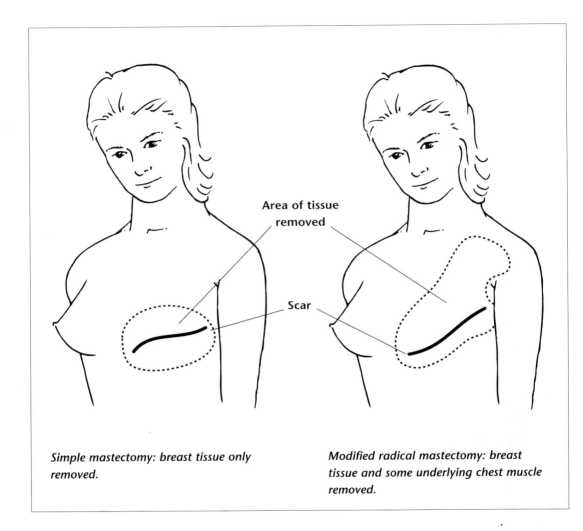

Area of tissue removed

Scar

Simple mastectomy: breast tissue only removed.

Modified radical mastectomy: breast tissue and some underlying chest muscle removed.

But there is little to choose between levels of anxiety following either operation.

Mastectomy can be the better option when:
- the tumour is in the centre of the breast or directly behind the nipple;
- the breast is small and would be distorted by a partial mastectomy;
- there are several cancerous areas in the breast;
- you would feel happier in yourself to 'have it all out';
- you have ductal carcinoma *in situ* (DCIS; see pages 40-1). Paradoxically this is the earliest cancer to be found and is highly unlikely to have become systemic (gone to other parts of

your body). If the whole breast is removed, your chance of cure is almost 100 per cent, but this is a drastic remedy for a cancer that might never spread or could be treated equally successfully by a less radical method. The trouble is that the doctors just will not know what is best until they have the results of a major trial now in progress comparing biopsy, irradiation and Tamoxifen in various combinations.

It is important for the doctors to establish whether the cancer has spread to your axillary lymph nodes. Surgeons are divided as to whether it is better to do an axillary sampling (removing a few nodes to test for spread) or an axillary clearance (removing the whole lot whether or not there is evidence of spread). Some doctors feel that to take a sample of, say, only four nodes when there are 30 in all is like

playing Russian roulette. If your doctor says that it is unnecessary to investigate your lymph nodes, you need to ask why.

A still-unresolved question is whether premenopausal women should be operated on in the second half of their menstrual cycle when their oestrogen levels are lower. Some studies suggest that this improves their survival rate. Ask your surgeon what he or she thinks.

 What are the side effects of surgery?

 Everyone reacts differently, but common symptoms are soreness in the chest area or tingling. The scar may feel tight and tender for a while. You may not be able to wear a bra or anything that puts pressure on the operated area. Your arm and shoulder on the operated side will feel stiff. (See page 54 for exercises.)

Radiotherapy

Radiotherapy is usually recommended after any form of partial mastectomy to reduce the risk of local recurrence (when the cancer comes back to the same place in the breast). It is sometimes done following a mastectomy but usually is not considered so necessary. If the armpit area has been cleared of lymph glands, you should not need irradiation there as well. Surgery and radiotherapy, particularly when both are applied to the armpit area, increase your risk of lymphoedema (a swollen arm; see page 57).

Questions you may want to ask your surgeon before an operation

● Can you tell me why you think the operation you are recommending to me is best for me?
● How disfiguring will it be?
● What are the immediate after-effects of this surgery?
● Can you tell from the type of tumour I have how likely I am to have a local recurrence? Or whether the cancer will spread?

Treatments for early breast cancer

 When will I have radiotherapy?

 When you have recovered from your operation; usually a few weeks later.

 What does it involve?

 You will first see the consultant radiotherapist who will explain the treatment: why you are having it, how it will be done and what your dosage will be. Ask all the questions you want. You will then spend some time in a simulator unit where the radiographer will measure the area to be irradiated and draw defining lines around it. All this takes time – an hour or more – but your treatment will last only a few minutes, each day at the same time.

 How often will I have it?

 Usually five days a week for four to six weeks. Treatment plans do vary.

 What are the side effects?

 Everyone is different, but a common one is a skin reaction – itching, soreness and a sensation rather like bad sunburn. The radiographer will advise you on skin care and healing creams. Always wear loose clothing, do not use any scented products and keep the treated area dry. You may feel very tired towards the end and for a few weeks after your treatment, so be kind to yourself. Try to find a friend who will drive you to your appointments and do not work so hard. Depression is not unusual.

 I've heard that there can be serious long-term side effects. What are they?

 Unfortunately, there are some. If the axilla is included in the radiotherapy field, lymphoedema is one (see page 57). Other, more rare problems can appear years later as a result of radiation damage to nerves or bones. These injuries are less likely to happen today because the dosage is lower and more carefully monitored. RAGE (see page 78) is an organization which supports women with radiotherapy damage. In the UK the Department of Health is issuing guidelines for doctors and factsheets for patients.

Chemotherapy and radiotherapy may both be prescribed on their own, or together, as primary treatment for breast cancer. This may be because either the type of cancer, or its advanced stage, makes the tumour inoperable. Some women whose tumour could be removed surgically wish to preserve their breast, if at all possible, and are prepared to try these options first. Some doctors (particularly in the USA) believe that more women with early breast cancer should be having chemotherapy as a primary treatment before surgery. Here are some reasons for this view:

● Chemotherapy shrinks the tumour.
● A smaller tumour is easier to remove and reduces the risk of scattering cancer cells during surgery.
● It enables doctors to assess how sensitive the cancer is to chemotherapy which will determine later treatment decisions.
● It is important to start systemic treatment immediately a cancer has been discovered.

Second-stage treatment

Systemic adjuvant therapy is the second stage of treatment offered to many women with early breast cancer. It takes two forms: chemotherapy and endocrine (hormone) therapy.

Chemotherapy

Chemotherapy uses a combination of anti-cancer (cytotoxic) drugs to kill the cancer cells. It may be given by tablet, injection or, still under trial, infusion. By this last method drugs are administered on a drip-feed principle through a narrow tube (Hickman line) inserted into the patient's chest.

 When should chemotherapy start?

 As soon as possible after diagnosis, certainly not later than four weeks.

 How long will it last?

 That depends partly on the type of cancer and what the doctor decides is the best combination of drugs for you. Medical opinion is still uncertain about the optimum duration, but it is unlikely to be less than three months or more than a year.

 Do I have to stay in hospital for my treatment?

 Chemotherapy is mostly done now on an outpatient basis and administered by a specialist nurse. You have a course which lasts so many cycles and is usually every three or four weeks.

Treatments for early breast cancer

 I have heard that there are awful side effects like losing all your hair, getting mouth ulcers and being terribly sick. Will this happen to me?

 Different drugs have different effects and the same dosage and combination can affect women quite differently. Many of these side effects are unpleasant, but there are ways of counteracting them. For instance, you can wear a cold cap to freeze the hair follicles before taking chemotherapy: then, although your hair may get thin, it will not all drop out. In all cases when the treatment stops the hair grows back. There are also anti-emetic drugs to stop you vomiting. You should always report your side effects so that the doctors can consider a different drug combination or dosage.

Endocrine therapy

Endocrine (hormone) therapy works by blocking oestrogen and so inhibiting cell growth. The drug used is Tamoxifen, of which 20mg must be taken daily for at least two years to achieve its effect. (Trials are in progress to decide on its optimum duration.) A useful book about this drug is *Tamoxifen and Breast Cancer* by Michael W. DeGregorio and Valerie J. Wiebe (Yale University Press, 1994).

Benefits of adjuvant therapy

A major overview of 133 breast cancer trials involving 75,000 women all over the world revealed that there was a significant advantage both in terms of survival and delayed recurrence for:

- premenopausal women who received chemotherapy;
- premenopausal women who had their ovaries removed;
- postmenopausal women given Tamoxifen;
- some postmenopausal women who had both chemotherapy and Tamoxifen – these did even better than the Tamoxifen-only group.

These simple conclusions broadly indicate the benefits of adjuvant therapy: in itself a big step forward, considering that there are many women still not being offered adjuvant therapy for early breast cancer in the UK. What the results cannot tell us with any precision is which patients in these two age spans did best with what drugs, administered for how long, and in what strength. There are, for instance, several cytotoxic drugs which can be used in different combinations for different types of tumour. They also interact differently with other treatments.

Tamoxifen is known to be effective in postmenopausal women with hormone-dependent (oestrogen-receptor-positive) breast cancer because of its anti-oestrogenic effect. However, it also benefits some younger women and some women with negative receptor status, suggesting that there may be other responsible mechanisms or factors, not yet fully understood.

We have to wait for further research – biological and clinical – before these questions can be fully answered. The Adjuvant Breast Cancer (ABC) Trial is one such study, now in progress at hospitals throughout the UK, which aims to test whether chemotherapy adds to the benefits of Tamoxifen for early breast cancer in all ages. It is well designed and you will be very well supervised should you decide to join it.

Two other major areas of investigation are:
● What should be offered to women with apparently very early breast cancer – no node involvement – yet some of whom will develop metastatic disease quite quickly.
● Whether all women with early-stage cancer should be offered much more aggressive chemotherapy at the beginning of their treatment, as happens more frequently in the USA.

Meanwhile doctors can make some reasonably confident assumptions about appropriate medication, provided that they have a detailed pathological analysis of the tumour. The importance of evaluating prognostic indicators has been briefly mentioned (page 41). These indicators are complex biological markers, too technical to describe here, but you should ask your medical team to explain in simple laywoman's language the special features of your cancer that lead them to recommend a particular kind of treatment.

I have heard about high-dose chemotherapy. What does this mean and to whom is it given?

This technique for early breast cancer was pioneered in the USA but is criticized by many British doctors for being unnecessarily aggressive. It is suitable only for women whose cancer is sensitive to chemotherapy. It is based on the theory that the larger the dose of chemotherapy, the more likely you are to kill all the cancer cells that may be lurking in the body. Before this treatment starts, certain blood cells, called periferal blood stem cells, are collected and removed, leaving the patient very vulnerable to life-threatening infection. As soon as the chemotherapy is completed – a matter of days – the collected blood stem cells are reintroduced into the patient's blood system to revive the immune system. This procedure can be repeated. Trials are currently being carried out in 13 centres around the UK.

What are clinical trials? How are they run?

Clinical trials are studies to discover which is the best treatment for a particular condition. Usually they are for drugs which have been through extensive earlier testing before they are tried on human patients, but they can and should be used to test other treatments like types of surgery, varying doses of radiotherapy and so on. To ensure that there is no bias, trials are randomized, which means the patient is randomly selected by a computer to enter a particular group or 'arm'. Drug trials are usually double blind – neither doctor nor patient knows what drug they are taking (or it could be a placebo, a dummy drug).

Treatments for early breast cancer

 Should I ask to join a trial? I have heard of informed consent. What does it mean?

 Start by asking your doctors whether they are participating in clinical trials – many of the bigger ones are run on a multicentre basis. If they are, that is a good sign, because it shows they want to keep up to date with developments in the treatment of breast cancer. However, no one should be entered into a trial without their knowledge and without giving their informed consent. This means fully understanding the purpose of the trial, why you are considered suitable for it and what it will mean for you. You should be given plenty of time to discuss your options, preferably with a medical person who is not involved in the trial, so cannot be thought to be trying to influence you. You should also ask for detailed written information.

Choosing to enter a trial means that you will not be able to choose your individual treatment. It does mean that you have a chance of receiving a new improved treatment and you may be helping to improve breast cancer treatment for future generations of women. But if, having thought about it carefully, you decide against entry, you should not feel guilty nor worried that your doctors will 'take it out' on you. Whatever your decision, if you are in a specialist breast unit you will be well looked after.

The decision is yours. An important condition of giving your informed consent is that you can always change your mind at a later date and decide to withdraw from the trial.

Chapter six
Taking care

'Every woman should have access to a specialist breast care nurse trained to give information and psychological support.'

(Fourth Macmillan minimum standard)

The breast care nurse

Before you have your operation a lot of questions will be racing through your mind. Some you will want to ask your doctor, but others you may find easier to talk over with the breast care nurse. For example: How am I going to look? How is this illness going to affect my life, my relationships? Will I still feel like a woman? Will I have to wear different clothes?

The breast care nurse is an indispensable member of the breast specialist team and you should be able to see her in either the assessment clinic or breast clinic when you are referred for the first time. She has specialist knowledge of breast cancer and is usually also a trained counsellor. She is there to answer the questions you may have forgotten to ask the doctors or perhaps did not think were important enough for them. Nothing will seem trivial to the breast care nurse. Everything you need is her concern and she will be there for you from the time of diagnosis and throughout your treatment. She may also come and visit you in your home.

Some operations, particularly for lumpectomy, may involve a short stay in hospital. A mastectomy of any kind will mean you have to stay in for a few days until the drains can be removed. The breast care nurse will talk to you about any problems you may be having.

Looking after yourself

Either the breast care nurse or the physiotherapist will show you some exercises which you should continue to do for some months after you return home, if not indefinitely. These exercises are particularly important if you also have radiotherapy.

Taking care

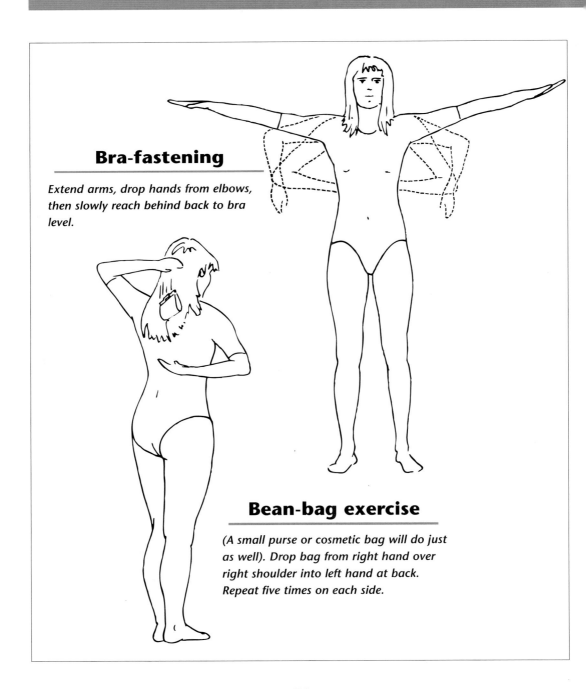

Bra-fastening

Extend arms, drop hands from elbows, then slowly reach behind back to bra level.

Bean-bag exercise

(A small purse or cosmetic bag will do just as well). Drop bag from right hand over right shoulder into left hand at back. Repeat five times on each side.

Arm-swinging

Place unaffected arm on back of chair and rest forehead on arm. Allow your other arm to hang loosely and swing from shoulder, forwards and backwards, then side to side and in small circles. As arm relaxes, increase length of swings and size of circles. Swing until arm is relaxed.

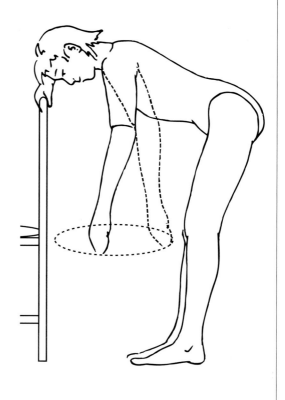

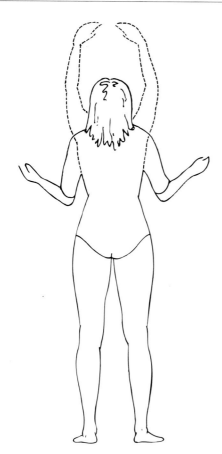

Wall-reaching

Feet apart for balance. Stand close to and facing wall. Start with hands at shoulder level and gradually work hands up the wall. Slide hands back to shoulder level before starting exercise again. Do slowly several times a day. Mark spot reached and aim higher each time.

Taking care

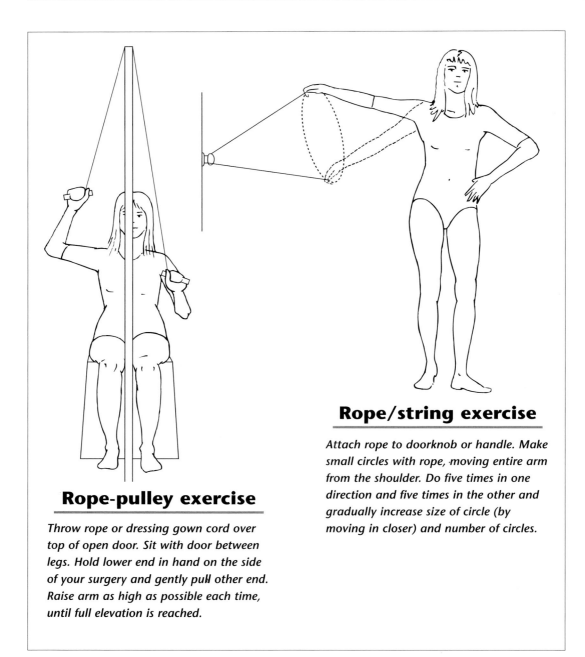

Rope-pulley exercise

Throw rope or dressing gown cord over top of open door. Sit with door between legs. Hold lower end in hand on the side of your surgery and gently pull other end. Raise arm as high as possible each time, until full elevation is reached.

Rope/string exercise

Attach rope to doorknob or handle. Make small circles with rope, moving entire arm from the shoulder. Do five times in one direction and five times in the other and gradually increase size of circle (by moving in closer) and number of circles.

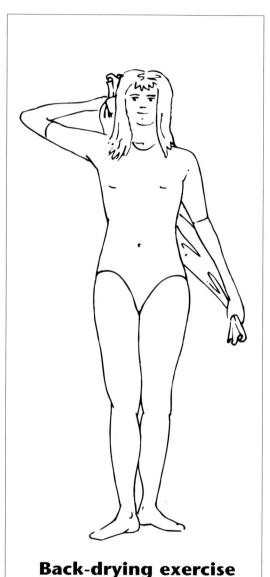

Back-drying exercise

With towel or similar item use a gentle back-drying motion. Reverse procedure.

The breast care nurse will also advise you on how to look after your hand and arm on the operated side. Lymphoedema (swollen arm) can become a chronic condition after surgery and radiotherapy. Here are some basic precautions to protect yourself:

● Go easy on heavy household jobs like vacuuming or moving furniture and on energetic sports using your arms until you are fully recovered.

● Be careful about heavy lifting.

● If your arm swells, keep it high whenever possible, especially at night on a pillow, and avoid having injections or your blood pressure taken in this arm.

● Wear gloves for gardening, washing up and any rough work. Use a thimble for sewing and an electric razor for underarm shaving.

● Any cut or scrape should be washed immediately, and an antiseptic applied. If it shows signs of infection or feels warm or swollen, report it without delay to your doctor or breast care nurse.

Taking care

Keep appointments; stay vigilant

You will be given appointments for check-up, every few months to start with, and then once a year. It is obviously important to keep these appointments, but if anything worries you in between times do not hesitate to ask for an appointment then.

It is quite natural at first to think that any twinge or pain means the cancer has come back. Most women find that they gradually become calmer and some will genuinely almost forget they ever had cancer. All the same, it is important to be vigilant and to take care of yourself. If you have had cancer in one breast, you are at much greater risk of having it in the second breast, so keep up your usual breast self-examination and go for screening if you are in the national programme. Report any unusual and/or persistent symptom as soon as possible. It could be a delayed side effect from one of your treatments or it may be something quite other than cancer, but whatever it is, your doctors should know about it as soon as possible.

Sometimes the cancer does come back to the same place, despite everything. This may require more surgery; however, as long as it is dealt with immediately it can usually be put right. Should the cancer spread, there is now an increasing number of drugs to deal with the problem. Many women with recurrent or

It is vital to keep your regular check-up appointments after your treatment is complete.

advanced cancer can still have long periods of remission (disease-free time). Nonetheless, recurrence will cause you and your family a lot of anxiety. There are organizations and self-help support groups which can help (see page 78), as well as the breast care nurse.

Alternative approaches

 Can complementary therapies help with cancer?

 Most certainly, and at any stage. Their benefit is psychological as well as physical. Aromatherapy, shiatsu and other types of gentle massage can be very relaxing. Meditation and visualization are techniques you may already know, but if you don't, you will not find them difficult to learn; they can help you cope with emotional stress. Homeopathic remedies can help alleviate nausea and other drug side effects. Some people find faith healing very rewarding. None of these therapies offers a cure for cancer, but then neither can conventional medicine.

What complementary medicine does do for many people with cancer is to make them feel more in control of their lives. You choose what you want to do. You discuss your needs with your therapist. You have the undivided attention of your therapist for at least an hour at a time – a luxury never available in even the best-run hospital, unless it is one of the enlightened few which are now inviting complementary therapists into their wards. And many nurses are training as aromatherapists.

 My doctor says complementary medicine is all quackery. Should I tell him or her what I'm doing?

 It's up to you. The doctor cannot stop you and it might open his or her mind a bit if he or she realizes that not only can you think for yourself but it seems to be doing you good!

 I've heard that there are special cancer diets? Should I go on one?

 'Proceed with caution' is probably the best advice. Some of them are very difficult to keep to and you may miss out on some essential nutrients. Another danger is that you may, without realizing it, become so obsessive that you feel unreasonably guilty if you cannot stick to it. Follow the dietary advice in Chapter three, making sure that you consume plenty of fruit and vegetables. Studies show that women who change to a low-fat diet after treatment for breast cancer have longer periods of remission. You probably felt well before your cancer diagnosis. Eat healthy food now to regain your strength.

Chapter seven

Looking good

Breast reconstruction

If you think you might want a breast reconstruction, it is a good idea to discuss the matter with your surgeon before your operation. You do not have to make a firm decision at this early stage, but if there is any chance you might want one, it will help the surgeon in the way he or she does your mastectomy. (Breast reconstruction is also possible for women having a lumpectomy.)

Doctors differ in their views about timing and methods of reconstruction: some prefer to do it at the same time as the mastectomy; others may advise their patients to wait a year or more to see how they feel. If you have had radiotherapy, you will certainly have to wait some months until the skin has completely recovered. Some breast surgeons prefer to delegate this operation to a plastic surgeon colleague who specializes in breast reconstruction.

What is breast reconstruction?

It is an operation to replace the breast tissue and restore the shape of the breast, matching as nearly as possible the remaining natural breast. Sometimes the surgeon will suggest reducing or lifting the other breast to match the 'new' one. There are several types of breast reconstruction (see the illustrations on pages 61–5). Some use a silicone implant on its own; others use your own muscle and fat, or a combination of both.

Your doctor will advise you on the one most suitable for you. Always ask the surgeon to show you pictures of the finished results of similar operations he or she has done. Some carry higher risks of complications and all these operations should be done only by experienced surgeons.

Subcutaneous mastectomy

In this operation the breast skin is preserved, including the nipple. A silicone implant replaces the breast tissue and the scar runs in the crease under the breast.
● **Advantage** Usually looks good and is simple to do, involving a short stay in hospital and a quick recovery.
● **Disadvantage** Carries risk of capsular contracture if the prosthesis is under the skin. This happens when fibrous scar tissue attaches to the implant, making it hard and painful. It may require another operation (explantation) to remove the implant, which can be replaced, and the capsule.

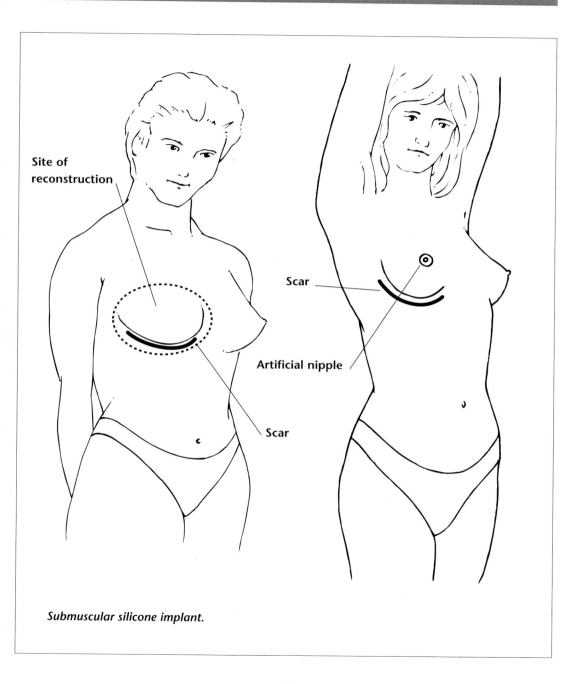

Site of
reconstruction

Scar

Artificial nipple

Scar

Submuscular silicone implant.

Looking good

Submuscular silicone implant

This is similar to the above operation, but the implant is placed in a deep pocket on top of the chest wall and under the pectoral (chest) muscle. The scar may follow the line of the mastectomy scar; preferably, it is in the crease of the breast. This operation is not possible for women who have had a radical mastectomy (they have no chest muscle) or are large-breasted or have had radiotherapy (their skin will not be sufficiently elastic).

● **Advantage** Looks good, particularly for a woman with small breasts. As easy a procedure as for an implant under the skin.

● **Disadvantage** The implant can alter shape slightly as the overlying muscle contracts.

Tissue expansion

Various tissue expansion methods are used, all based on the principle that an inflatable silicone bag (or deflated permanent silicone prosthesis) is inserted under the chest muscle. Over a period of two months the bag is gently expanded by injecting a sterile saline solution through a valve under local anaesthetic until the new breast is slightly larger than the natural breast. If the bag method is used, it will be removed three months later – to allow for the stretched skin to assume a natural droop – to be substituted by a permanent silicone prosthesis. Alternatively, if the permanent prosthesis has already been inserted, just the valve will be removed.

● **Advantage** A gentle method and the time it takes is compensated for by a good cosmetic result in most cases.

● **Disadvantage** It is not always suitable for women who have had radical surgery or radiotherapy for the same reasons as above: the skin is not sufficiently elastic.

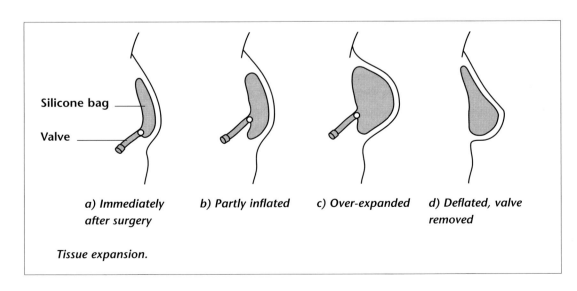

Silicone bag

Valve

a) Immediately after surgery

b) Partly inflated

c) Over-expanded

d) Deflated, valve removed

Tissue expansion.

Muscle and skin flap rotation

There are two ways in which this operation may be done:

Method 1

A flap of muscle and skin on the back directly behind the operated breast is rotated and tunnelled just below the armpit and placed on the chest wall. The new skin supplements what is already on the chest to create an envelope for the muscle which can, if necessary, be bulked out further with a silicone implant placed behind it to match the size of the other breast. Scarring consists of a horizontal or diagonal scar on the back and a neat oval scar round the breast.

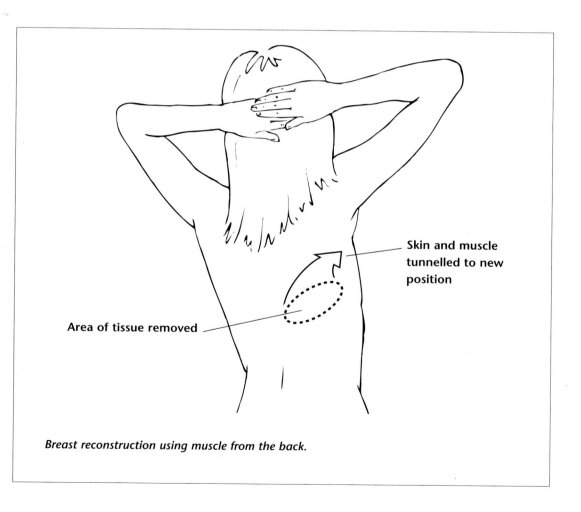

Skin and muscle tunnelled to new position

Area of tissue removed

Breast reconstruction using muscle from the back.

Looking good

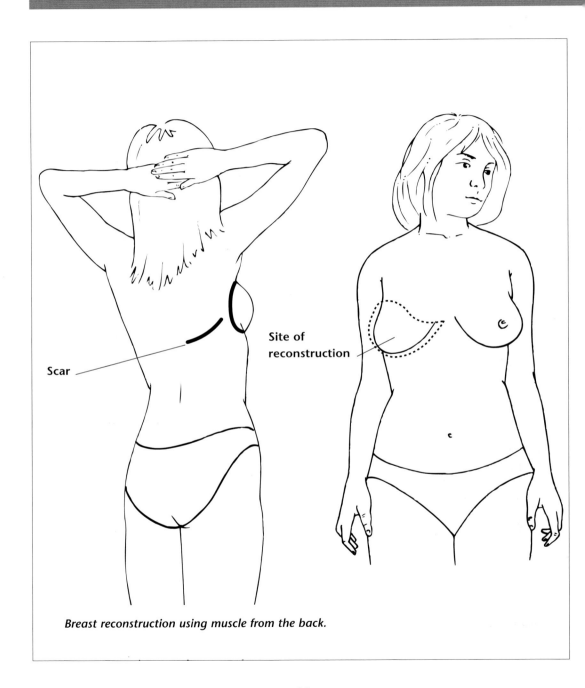

Scar

Site of
reconstruction

Breast reconstruction using muscle from the back.

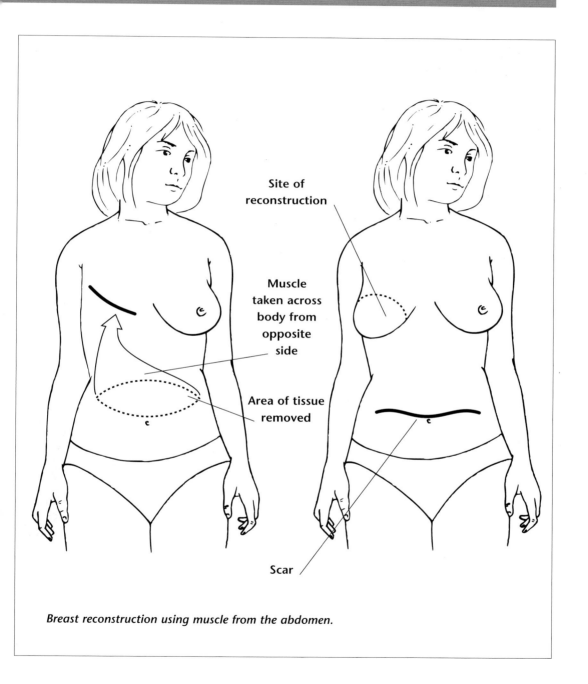

Site of
reconstruction

Muscle
taken across
body from
opposite
side

Area of tissue
removed

Scar

Breast reconstruction using muscle from the abdomen.

Looking good

Method 2

A flap of muscle and skin taken from the abdominal muscle, which runs up from the pubic bone to the breastbone, is rotated and tunnelled upwards to the breast area. There is usually enough tissue here to match a large breast without needing an additional silicone implant. Scarring on the abdomen can be vertical or horizontal; on the breast it will be oval.

● **Advantage** Both these operations are possible for women who have had a radical mastectomy or radiotherapy (or both). The transferred tissue is well supplied with blood vessels which aid healing.

● **Disadvantages** Both are major operations involving at least a week in hospital. Method 1 carries less risk of complications but does require an implant in most cases. Method 2 has a very high complication rate, even in skilled hands, and many surgeons are now concerned that the risks outweigh the benefits.

 What about my nipple? Can that be reconstructed too?

 It is possible, but usually it is done a few months after the breast reconstruction when the breast has settled into its permanent position. This enables the surgeon to line up the new nipple with the one on your other breast. The operation involves a skin graft using skin from behind your ear or part of your other nipple. Skin for the areola (dark circle round the nipple) is usually taken from the groin. The long-term results are often far from perfect. You could consider the effective alternative of a stick-on nipple which can either be individually moulded to match your other one (expensive) or bought ready-made (inexpensive).

 What exactly are silicone implants? Aren't they dangerous? I've heard they are banned in America.

 Breast implants are made of silicone gel encased in a thin silicone envelope. Held in the hand an implant feels soft and mobile like a real breast. They have been used for years for breast augmentation and were very popular until there were reports of ruptures, leaking and infections. Some women believe that they have contracted cancer and certain sorts of auto-immune disease as a result. For a short time the American Food and Drug Association (FDA) banned their use. Now they are allowed, but only for women in clinical studies. In the UK a group of doctors commissioned by the Department of Health to investigate has concluded that there is insufficient evidence to stop using them. From now on all breast implant operations are being recorded in a central registry. Meanwhile research is continuing to find a safer, more compatible material for implants.

Breast prosthesis

Some women will feel that reconstruction is not, and never will be, an option for them. A breast prosthesis, or breast form as it is more easily called, may not be something you particularly want to think about before your operation. The breast care nurse will discuss it with you when you feel ready and bring you some samples to show you what to expect. As the eighth Macmillan standard states, 'Every woman should have a sensitive and complete breast prosthesis fitting service, where appropriate.'

What does a breast prosthesis look like?

These days, it is available in an extensive range of shapes, sizes and skin colours. They are made of soft, anatomically shaped silicone which reproduces the natural curves of a woman's breast, including, if she wants it, her nipple outline. The surface feels soft and smooth. The underside of a prosthesis is more variable. It can be firm, or soft and pliable. A woman who has had a lot of chest tissue removed and has a hollowing on her chest wall may prefer a firm underside to give her shape, while a woman with an irregular scar may like a softer underside which will mould to her chest wall.

Held in the hand, a breast prosthesis initially may feel rather cold and heavy, but it swiftly warms up with body contact and the sense of weight disappears once it is inside your bra and held against your chest wall. A well-fitting prosthesis restores your balance as well as your shape. It will never look or feel exactly like your real breast, but you can be reassured that a well-chosen prosthesis worn in an appropriate bra will match the shape of your natural breast. *The world outside will not know the difference.*

When do I get a breast prosthesis?

Whether you have had a mastectomy or a lumpectomy, you will not be able to wear anything that puts pressure on your scar and the surrounding area for six to eight weeks. A bra is too constricting for many women during this period. You may prefer to wear a camisole top or a seamless cotton vest which, if it has lycra in it, will give you some support.

Even after the scar has fully healed you may be having further treatment such as radiotherapy which tends to make the skin tender and sore for a while. Until this sensitivity has completely disappeared it will not be possible for you to wear an ordinary prosthesis.

Your breast care nurse will be able to fit you with a lightweight temporary prosthesis, made of a synthetic washable fibre encased in cotton,

Looking good

Types of breast prostheses.

which you can wear inside your bra. Many women continue to use these lightweight prostheses when they want to feel relaxed at home yet safe from being caught 'undressed' by an unexpected caller.

 Do I have to pay for a breast prosthesis?

 If you are treated on the NHS you will be fitted with a free prosthesis. This can be replaced when it wears out – prostheses are normally guaranteed for two years – or you may need a new one if you lose or gain weight. Either ask your consultant to give you a surgical appliance form when you go for your check-up or, if you have moved or no longer attend hospital for check-ups, ask your family doctor to write to your local breast cancer surgeon to send you the form. This can be taken to the surgical appliance office at the hospital or to an approved stockist or fitter.

If you have had private treatment, you may find that you are not given much advice or help after your operation. Some private health insurance schemes will pay up to £100 for the first prosthesis. If you later go back on the NHS for follow-up, you can obtain further prostheses, as you need them, free of charge. However, if you decide to remain with private health care, you will have to buy your prostheses from a specialist shop or through mail order. Prostheses cost anything upwards of £70 to £200 and they are VAT exempted.

 Who does the fitting?

 The breast care nurse is the ideal person, but if there is not one in your hospital, the fitter could be a ward nurse who will have had no special training or an appliance officer who deals with all types of prosthesis fitting. Even today the appliance officer is sometimes a man. Sometimes the fitter is a representative from a prosthesis manufacturer. She will be well trained, but she will show you only her company's products.

 How do I choose the right prosthesis?

 Size and shape are important, but so is achieving a matching skin tone, especially for black women. Find a sheer nylon stocking of the same tone as the skin on your chest (not your leg, which is usually darker) and take it with you to your hospital fitting. There are some off-the-shelf prostheses in various skin tones or you can have one tinted, free of charge if you are an NHS patient.

In theory a woman is entitled to the prosthesis of her choice on the NHS (there are more than 40 different types available); in practice she will be lucky if she is shown more than two or three. Lack of storage space and a

Looking good

restrictive purchasing policy are some of the reasons for this meagre choice. One way of getting round this problem is to send off for free catalogues from the manufacturers: you can show them to your breast care nurse or appliance officer. Or arrange with Breast Cancer Care for a free fitting with an experienced fitter who will show you the full range for your needs.

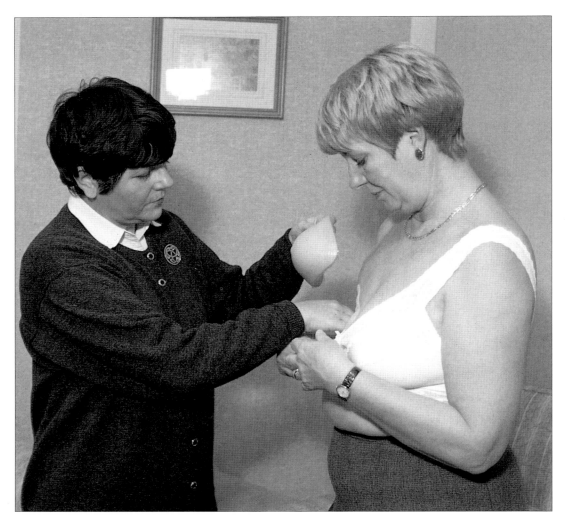

A breast prosthesis fitting.

I've heard that there is a self-supporting prosthesis. Could I wear one?

 Self-supporting prostheses are particularly successful for women who have had a bilateral mastectomy (both breasts removed). They are attached to adhesive velcro strips stuck to the chest wall. They feel secure and move with the body. They can be worn for up to ten days, at night as well, and in the bath or shower. The natural oils in your skin will gradually break down the adhesive and the velcro strip then peels away easily and painlessly.

Some women prefer to remove the prosthesis at night but leave the skin support in place so that the prosthesis can be easily reattached in the morning. When wet, you simply pat the prosthesis dry as you would your own breast. Self-supporting prostheses are available in all sizes, but a large-breasted woman may find the size and weight uncomfortable.

Always take medical advice before you consider wearing one and always test the adhesive on your chest wall beforehand. It may not be suitable if you have had radiotherapy.

 I have had a partial mastectomy which has changed the shape of my breast. Is there anything I can do about it?

 You could have a shell which is hollow-backed and fits over the operated breast, restoring it to its original contour. Or you may need no more than a small wedge fitted around the operation site to fill out the bottom or side of your bra.

 Can I have a nipple on my prosthesis?

 There are some very good prostheses with nipples. If you want something more pronounced, you can buy the stick-on variety described on page 66.

 What should I bring to a fitting?

 Wear a plain T-shirt without patterns or pockets so that you can be sure you choose a prosthesis which gives you a smooth outline. You may also want to bring a favourite bra, a swimsuit or a low-necked dress or blouse which you would like to be able to continue wearing. Many women like to bring a friend or relative along to discuss their various choices. This is the opportunity to get what is right for you.

Looking good

What should I expect at a fitting?

There should be an ample choice of bras and prostheses. The room should be light and reasonably spacious with a full-length mirror so that you have enough room to look at yourself from all angles. You need privacy, no interruptions and time to discuss your requirements. The fitter will ask you whether you have had any problems following your treatment and she will want to know about your lifestyle so that she can make appropriate suggestions. Some fitters are happy to advise you on ways of adapting your wardrobe.

I love swimming and aerobics. Will I still be able to do these things?

You can buy special foam prostheses for swimming, but unless you are very active it is probably not necessary. Many women find that a prosthesis cut out of foam rubber is adequate. Tennis players, golfers and other especially athletic women may prefer to wear a lightweight prosthesis.

You can enjoy aerobics and other activities while wearing a prosthesis – it is undetectable.

Models at a Breast Cancer Care fashion show prove the point that you can look great after breast surgery.

Looking good

Do I have to wear a special bra with my prosthesis?

There are specially made mastectomy bras with a pocket in the cup to hold the prosthesis. If you are good with your needle, you can sew in tapes or pockets inside the cup of an ordinary bra. You can do the same inside the cup of a favourite swimsuit. A few hospitals will pay for this to be done.

Whatever bra you choose, and there are plenty of suitable ones in department and chain stores, make sure that it fits you properly. It is surprising how often women wear bras that are too small for them. If you are in any doubt, go to a good department store where there is a trained bra fitter, preferably one who knows about prosthesis fitting as well.

Time to adjust

It will take time to adjust to wearing a prosthesis. Some women find that they never can and either do without or have a breast reconstruction. Other women decide right from the start that they will not wear a breast prosthesis. These are individual decisions and you must take the one that makes you feel most comfortable, psychologically as well as physically. Do not feel pressured by outside influences. Do what suits you.

Looking good makes you feel better. With a little ingenuity, and even if you have to change your bra, you will probably find that you can wear most, if not all the clothes in your wardrobe. Do not make the mistake so many women do and give away favourite things before your operation.

Breast Cancer Care has been running fashion shows around the country for several years, always using as models women who have had surgery for breast cancer. They look marvellous and they are an inspiration to the large audiences (mainly women of all ages who have had breast cancer) because they show how it is perfectly possible to wear nice clothes and look good after breast cancer – as good as you always did. Looking good makes you feel good.

Chapter eight

Living with breast cancer

The woman who has had breast cancer has to find her own way of absorbing the experience into her life. No one can tell her what she ought to do or how she ought to feel. None of us knows how we will react to a crisis or how we will cope with the after-effects, particularly when it is a life-threatening experience like cancer. Our personality affects our reaction.

One woman will find that she can cope best by putting the whole experience behind her as quickly as possible. Denial is her weapon and she may almost pretend that it has never happened. Another will have a strong fighting spirit, determined to beat the cancer, come what may, by every means possible. She will read everything, try anything and seek help from wherever she can find it. Her complete opposite is the woman who accepts what is happening and asks few questions. Each of us has to fight our personal battle with the best weapons we can muster.

Many women find that in the crisis of breast cancer their whole life alters. Their values change and former ambitions may fade. Relationships change, often becoming stronger, particularly within a family, but sometimes they wither and die. Friends who are afraid of cancer for themselves may drop out of your life. You make new friends through your illness.

Sex can become a problem, made more difficult because it is hard to talk about. It is not just the mutilation of losing a breast that can cause a woman to wonder whether she will still be loved and desirable. The side effects of chemotherapy and radiotherapy can be very debilitating. Libido can vanish and the quality of life become very tenuous for a while. It is not surprising that one-third of women with breast cancer suffer clinical depression for at least a year after treatment.

Do not be ashamed to seek psychiatric help if you need it. Your breast care nurse will help you, but if you are not lucky enough to have one, ask your doctor to refer you to a clinical psychologist or psychiatrist. Help is available and you owe it to yourself and those who love you to ask for it.

Sometimes it helps just to talk to someone who can give you practical advice or emotional support or just be quietly there for you, at the end of a telephone line, at times when you feel desperate and very lonely. Remember the ninth Macmillan standard: 'Every woman should have the opportunity to meet a former breast cancer patient who has been trained to offer support.'

More than twenty years ago Betty Westgate realized how important it was for women with

Living with breast cancer

breast cancer to be able to talk to each other about their experience. She had breast cancer in the days when it was a taboo subject and some women lived and died without telling their husband or their children what was wrong with them. Today the organization she founded, now called Breast Cancer Care, has more than 350 trained volunteers all around the UK who are available at the end of a telephone line for anyone who would like their help. A Breast Cancer Care volunteer is trained to listen and to give practical help. She can put you in touch with other sources of help and you can talk to her confidentially about concerns she will understand but which you may find hard to share even with your nearest and dearest. All Breast Cancer Care volunteers have had breast cancer themselves and are at least two years post-diagnosis and treatment.

Breast cancer can devastate a family. Partners, and children may find their lives turned upside down, but to whom can they turn for help? Men often feel helpless and left out as they watch their partner struggling through her treatment, but are not sure if they can cope themselves. They may be finding it difficult to deal with the practical problems or be worrying about revealing their own feelings in case that makes it harder for everyone to carry on.

The Partner Volunteer Service is a new Breast Cancer Care service which operates in a similar way to their Volunteer Service. All the Partner Volunteers are trained and have been through the experience of living with someone who has breast cancer. They offer the same mix of practical informative help and emotional support to any man who rings requesting help.

The organizations listed at the end of this book all provide skilled help and support, free of charge. As the tenth Macmillan standard states: 'Every woman should have information on all support services available to patients with breast cancer and their families.'

A trained Breast Cancer Care nurse offers welcome support and advice to a patient.

Useful addresses

Breast Cancer Care
Kiln House
210 New King's Road
London SW6 4NZ
Tel: 0171 384 2344
Nationwide Freeline:
0500 245345
Glasgow Helpline:
0141 353 1050
Edinburgh Helpline:
0131 221 1407
Services include
information, free leaflets,
free prosthesis fitting
service and volunteer
contacts.

BACUP
3 Bath Place
Rivington Street
London EC2A 3JR
Cancer Information
Services: Freephone
0800 181199
Counselling Service:
0171 696 9000
Free publications on all
aspects of cancer.

Bristol Cancer Help Centre
Grove House
Cornwallis Grove
Bristol BS8 4PG
Tel: 0117 947 3216
Offers emotional support,
complementary therapies
and self-help techniques
which can be used at
home alongside
treatment recommended
by the patient's doctors.
No one is turned away
for inability to pay.

CancerLink
17 Britannia Street
London WC1X 9JN
London Helpline:
0171 833 2451
Asian Support Line:
0171 713 7867
MACline for young
people: 0800 591 028
Edinburgh Helpline:
0131 228 5557
Information and support
by telephone or letter.
Free publications.
Resource for 500 cancer
support and self-help
groups.

Cancer Relief Macmillan Fund
15/19 Britten Street
London SW3 3TZ
Supports and develops
services for people with
cancer at every stage of
their illness.

Europa Donna
c/o **Cancerkin**
Royal Free Hospital
London NW3 2QG
Pan-European
organisation aiming
to inform all women
about breast cancer and
to campaign for better
standards of care. Free
newsletter.

Institute for Complementary Medicine
PO Box 194
London SE16 1QZ
Supplies names of
qualified recommended
practitioners of various
kinds of complementary
therapies. Send SAE
stating areas of interest.

RAGE (Radiotherapy Action Group Exposure)
Wellington House
Dixter Road, Northiam
East Sussex TN31 6LB
Tel: 01797 252956
Campaigns for recognition
of radiotherapy damage
and better treatments.

The National Cancer Alliance
PO Box 579
Oxford OX4 1LP
Tel: 01865 793566
An alliance of patients
and health professionals,
their relatives and
friends. Has published a
Directory of Cancer
Specialists in the UK.

Women's Nationwide Cancer Control Campaign
Suna House
128-130 Curtain Road,
London EC2A 3AR
Helpline: 0171 729 2229
Encourages measures for
the prevention and early
detection of cancer in
women and produces
a wide range of leaflets
and posters.

Overseas useful addresses

Australia

Queensland Cancer Fund
William Rudder House
PO Box 201
Springhill
Queensland
Tel: 612 257 1155

Canada

The Cancer Society
Canadian Cancer Centre
77 Bloor Street
Suite 1702
Toronto
Ontario M58 3A1
Tel: 416 975 5585

New Zealand

Breast Cancer Support Service
121 Moxham Avenue
Wellington 3
Tel: 644 863 349

Republic of South Africa

National Cancer Association of South Africa
9 Jubilee Road
Parktown
PO Box 2000
Johannesburg
Tel: 11 433 3900

USA

The National Breast Cancer Coalition
PO Box 66373
Washington DC 20035
Tel: 202 296 7477
A grassroots advocacy effort. Information, support.

Index